GETTING CASTANEDA

UNDERSTANDING CARLOS CASTANEDA

PETER LUCE

For Sri, Komang, Alex and Tommy

CONTENTS

Acknowledgments   vii
Bibliography   ix

1. Pablito's Mother   1
2. Why Read Castaneda?   5
3. Power Plants   20
4. Emanations of Intent   32
5. With the Dons in the Desert   42
6. Throwing the Other Self   56
7. Finding the Other Self Again   71
8. Dreaming Together   82
9. Cocoons and Filaments   96
10. Conservatives and Liberals   110
11. Lost in a Dream   119
12. Coming Down in L.A   139
13. A Yaqui Conclusion   149
14. Grandfather and Antoine   154
15. Twelve Books, Thirty Years   162

References   173
About the Author   175

ACKNOWLEDGMENTS

Thanks to the Editor, Leslie Caplan; Consultant and Proof-reader, Paul Greenway; and Designer, Sri Luce Rusna.

BIBLIOGRAPHY

Castaneda's Published Works

Book 1

Castaneda, Carlos. 1968. *The Teachings of Don Juan: A Yaqui Way of Knowledge*

Book 2

Castaneda, Carlos. 1971. *A Separate Reality: Further Conversations with Don Juan*

Book 3

Castaneda, Carlos. 1972. *Journey to Ixtlan: The Lessons of Don Juan*

Book 4

Castaneda, Carlos. 1974. *Tales of Power*

Book 5

Castaneda, Carlos. 1977. *The Second Ring of Power*

Book 6

Castaneda, Carlos. 1981. *The Eagle's Gift*

Book 7

Castaneda, Carlos. 1984. *The Fire from Within*
Book 8
Castaneda, Carlos. 1987. *The Power of Silence*
Book 9
Castaneda, Carlos. 1993. *The Art of Dreaming*
Book 10
Castaneda, Carlos. 1998. *Magical Passes*
Book 11
Castaneda, Carlos. 1998. *The Wheel of Time*
Book 12
Castaneda, Carlos. 1999. *The Active Side of Infinity*

1

PABLITO'S MOTHER

To see what you're up against if you want to understand Carlos Castaneda, consider this episode. Castaneda said it was a true story, it really happened.

He didn't give an exact date; it was sometime in 1974 or 1975. He had just published his fourth book, *Tales of Power*. At the end of it he described jumping off a cliff, the act that ended his apprenticeship with the sorcerer, don Juan. But after writing the book, he felt confused. He said he went back to Mexico to find out what really happened to him.

He decided to go to Pablito's house first. Pablito, his co-apprentice, had been with him on the plateau that day in 1973. Whatever happened there, they had been together.

Arriving about noon, he drove all the way around the village to avoid being seen. Something was different, though. The footpath was widened to a road now; he could drive right up to the front yard. The house had a new façade and a huge dog was sitting in front.

Pablito's mother, dona Soledad, burst out the door. They had nicknamed her 'Mrs Pyramid' in honor of her big backside and pointed head. But now she was suddenly thin and shapely, and looked twenty years younger! She greeted him directly, then put her fists on her hips and stood facing him, showing herself to him, exuding the power of a young girl, with a gleam in her eye. She boldly put her arm through his; he felt her breast push against him as they walked from his car.

She told him that Pablito had gone away for a few days. He asked about don Juan; she said he was gone forever and would never come back. She said don Juan had given her instructions for when Castaneda returned. She ordered him to come to her room.

Castaneda was freaking out and wanted to leave, but he followed Soledad into her room. 'You and I are the same,' she said, and sat on the edge of the bed. When he didn't respond, she stood up, dropped her skirt, and caressed her pubic area. 'You and I are one here! You know what to do!' Despite his alarm, Castaneda was incapable of looking away and stared at her new, youthful body.

He snapped to and decided he'd better just get out of there, so he mumbled some apologies and went to his car. He opened the trunk to unload some gifts to drop off. As he leaned in, he felt a huge furry hand grip the back of his neck.

He screamed and fell to the ground. Dona Soledad was a few feet away, shrugging her shoulders with an apologetic half-smile. Castaneda wondered how he could have been so stupid to once again come to Mexico and let himself fall into 'a bottomless pit'.

She then lurched and clawed at him, with clenched teeth. He kicked her, then threw himself over the car, but she grabbed his foot. They fell to the ground. The enormous dog joined the fight.

Castaneda ran inside and bolted the door; he heard the dog mauling the screaming dona Soledad. He suddenly realized what a stupid move he'd just made, as if he were 'running away from an ordinary opponent who could be shut out by simply closing a door'. Now he was locked in the house while the witch and her hound were between him and his car!

He let Soledad into the house, bleeding and torn and screaming about what 'that son of a bitch dog' had done to her. Castaneda made a dash for the car, got into the driver's seat, started the engine, and threw it into reverse. He turned to look over his shoulder, and came face to face with the dog, snapping and drooling.

He barely escaped to the roof of the car again. He slid around, trying to lure the animal out of one door so he could jump in through the other. Soledad was watching from the house, laughing, naked above the waist. Castaneda managed to pause at this moment to watch her breasts 'shaking with the convulsions of her laughter'. He was known as a ladies' man, and she was playing him. He went back into the house.

Dona Soledad, now calm, said that it was hopeless for him to try to escape, or for her to try to hold him there. The two of them were brought together for a purpose and neither could leave until it was finished. She promised to explain herself truthfully and answer honestly anything he asked.

Back in her room, Castaneda took out his notepad and wrote. She gave him her full life story and her history with don Juan. He asked about the other apprentices, male and female, who they were, and what they thought of him. This went on for five or six hours, until it got too dark to take notes.

As night fell, she prepared two warm tubs of scented water and they each washed up. The bath made him feel numb and tingly. Next thing, he was lying on top of her. He knew he was in danger, yet something was holding him there.

Castaneda recalled don Juan telling him that 'our great enemy is the fact that we never believe what is happening to us'. He slowly realized dona Soledad had wrapped her hair band around his neck and was choking him 'with great force and expertise'.

2

WHY READ CASTANEDA?

Carlos Castaneda's famous books about his sorcery apprenticeship with don Juan are generally considered to be part of the counterculture movement of the 1960s. When we hear Castaneda's name, we think of the themes of those times: rebellion, civil rights, free speech, the sexual revolution, self-awareness, new-age spirituality, Woodstock, hippies, and, of course, marijuana, LSD, and other psychedelic drugs.

Castaneda's early writing was about peyote, mushrooms and other 'power plants'. That focus contributed greatly to his success in the late sixties and early seventies in the USA. His books were grouped with the popular works of Aldous Huxley, Timothy Leary, Ken Kesey and other writers of that particular genre. For them, LSD and other psychotropic drugs provided a way for humanity to open the doors of perception and expand its awareness into a brighter future full of peace and love. There was also a movement towards esoteric Eastern religions, especially Hinduism and Buddhism with their meditation and yoga traditions promising inner peace. The Beatles had become world-famous singing about these themes, and it seemed they summed it up when they sang "all you need is love".

In the end, though, Castaneda was not about that at all. As the episode in the first chapter shows, his exoticism was not calm and soothing, or even Alice-in-Wonderland kind of strange. It was dark and dangerous, borderline crazy, very farfetched yet still somehow compelling. There was no carefree ride to a wonderful future through expanded awareness with Castaneda. It was more like being whooshed away and then hurled into a dangerous place somewhere, alone. You have no idea where you are. You don't remember where you came from, or how to get back. If you survive, you learn something.

He is associated with the "new age" self-help literature that started in the sixties and seventies, as well. Castaneda's work was widely misinterpreted this way. After his books became so successful, numbers of books by other authors appeared promoting supposedly Native American traditions of healing, health and spiritual wellbeing. But Castaneda actually said the self should be curtailed and erased, not repaired and improved. To him, too much concern with self-pity and self-presentation was the main characteristic of modern man, and the crucial challenge for mankind to face in order to survive and go forward.

These misinterpretations get in the way of seeing and understanding what Castaneda actually wrote about in his work. He wrote twelve books, published over thirty years between 1968 and 1998.

There are also issues of academic, journalistic and literary honesty raised by Castaneda's work. During his life, he claimed, untenably, that his books were autobiographical, that he really met don Juan and was trained as a sorcerer, and that he himself was a sorcerer leading a group of cohorts in a modern sorcery quest. These issues are real problems with Castaneda, and unsolvable. Having these unresolved questions about his basic integrity works against getting at the writing itself. We need to have a solution to this problem, even if it is also unprovable, so we can get around it and look at the work itself.

***

Who was Carlos Castaneda, really?

According to his books, Carlos Castaneda was an anthropology student at UCLA who made repeated trips to the Southwest USA to "collect information on the medicinal plants used by the Indians of the area", starting around 1960.

He met Juan Matus, known as "don Juan," a 70-year old Yaqui Indian who not only knew about medicinal herbs like peyote and datura but was also a sorcerer descended from a tradition of shamanism and magic that originated in Central Mexico more than 8,000 years ago.

These original sorcerers of ancient Mexico had been displaced by conquering groups in ancient times, and then brought to the point of extinction by the invading Spaniards and the Inquisition. Their sorcery tradition evolved over thousands of years into something more modern. Don Juan had a group of sixteen 20th century cohorts who pursued this modern form and called themselves the "new seers."

Castaneda became their apprentice and spent thirteen years learning sorcery from them in Mexico, from 1960 to 1973, and then another twenty-five years trying to establish his own sorcery group in Mexico and Los Angeles. He wrote twelve books describing his adventures and explaining his training. He died in 1998.

According to Castaneda's account, the sixteen sorcerers who trained him to become a new seer used a teaching method they inherited from antiquity. They utilized a form of awareness they called the "second attention."

Learning while in the second attention is similar to having experiences while under hypnosis or certain types of anesthesia. The old teachers could induce this state in Castaneda, like a hypnotist hypnotizing a patient. While Castaneda was in that state, which they also called "heightened awareness," he would feel incredibly lucid and totally suggestible.

While Castaneda was in heightened awareness his teachers taught him all the age-old secrets of sorcery and he immediately understood what he was taught. That learning would be faithfully stored somewhere in his mind or body, but when his lesson was completed he would have to be brought out of heightened awareness and returned to normal.

Just as a subject of hypnosis, when he returns to normal, forgets everything that happened while under hypnosis, and as anesthetized patients who are aware during their operation will not remember anything later, a student who is taught in heightened awareness also forgets everything when he returns to normal awareness. He not only forgets what he learned, he also forgets that he was even in that altered state and who was with him. He loses track of that segment of time in his life.

Castaneda says it's impossible to fully learn about sorcery while we are in our normal state of mind. Too much of it goes against common sense and rationality. In our normal state of mind, we may accept sorcery concepts in a theoretical way only, which doesn't make the knowledge usable to us except as a topic for conversation.

In the first five of Castaneda's books, he only knows about and talks about two sorcery teachers - don Juan and his assistant don Genaro. But there were sixteen elders responsible for his apprenticeship from the beginning to the end. They used their ability to manipulate heightened awareness so that Castaneda, in his normal state of mind, never remembered his fourteen other teachers. They taught him everything he needed to learn to master their system of knowledge and then made him forget it, and even forget that he had been with them.

They left him with the task of remembering them and all the teachings on his own, to claim that knowledge as his own personal power. This type of remembering is similar to recovering lost events from early childhood in psychotherapy. For sorcerers in don Juan's tradition it is done through special techniques of dreaming.

Castaneda said it took him more than twenty years to remember most but not all of what he had been taught. During that time he wrote his books composed of his direct recollections combined with his emerging memories, as he progressively recovered more and more.

In the early stages, don Juan gave him hallucinogenic plants to eat and smoke, to jolt him out of his initial lethargic condition, but that was only a very small part of Castaneda's overall experience. While writing his first two books he assumed that his experiences with the plants was paramount, and so did readers who only read his early books.

***

To understand what Castaneda said in his twelve books, and he did have a coherent message that was both complex and consistent on all levels, I will approach on several paths. I'll go through the books one by one, and date them. Noting the chronology of historical and literary events and how they interwove helps in understanding what happened. I'll recap some of the stories he told and introduce some of the main characters to bring new readers up to speed and to remind old readers. Then, I'll elucidate his underlying philosophy, and show that there is a completely consistent structure of concepts which run through all the books from start to finish.

It wouldn't be effective to simply explain Castaneda's philosophy in an essay. If I tried, the explanation would go something like this: Castaneda says the first attention must become aware of the second attention by remembering it – then you have access to the totality of your being and your awareness. But you're unlikely to survive the attempt.

It's much more effective to reveal it step by step in a story. This is what Castaneda did, and how it was revealed to him. It took Castaneda thirty years to report his journey through this learning. He didn't understand it at first, or in the middle, and possibly got parts of it wrong until the end. Meanwhile, he confused his readers, and probably himself too, with his personal life and pursuits. But everything is there in the books. It just needs to be distilled in a critical literary review.

I HAD a close encounter with Castaneda. On a cold late evening in Philadelphia in 1969 or 1970 I was walking past a lecture hall at my university with some friends. Somebody said, "Carlos Castaneda's in there giving a talk. It's almost over now". I had a vague idea who he was. I had read some reviews of his book; it had something to do with peyote eating and the discovery of an authentic, living Mexican sorcerer. Reportedly, Castaneda dressed like a businessman, in suit and tie, when he gave speeches about psychedelics and spirituality, which was an oddity. I was too late, though, so I walked back to my room and continued studying.

It wasn't until 1973, the year after I graduated, that I got around to reading Castaneda. I started with *A Separate Reality*, his second book, and then in 1975 I read the fourth book, *Tales of Power*. By the end of that book, Castaneda said he leapt from a 600-foot cliff. He reported that he did this in 1973 at the end of his 13-year apprenticeship with the awesome sorcerer don Juan, in Mexico.

It seemed to me the story was all about hallucinogenic drugs, another in a long line of books extolling drug-induced wisdom written in that era. There was no report on what happened after the leap, but obviously the writer lived to write more books.

Over the next 25 years, I followed him as he released book after book. Critical reactions to Castaneda, the man and his work, were all over the place; he was highly praised and highly condemned. Some said his writing was among the most important ever published in the history of anthropology, because he was getting information about Neolithic beliefs of a pre-literate civilization directly from a survivor of that era. Others said it was a hoax, fiction, and there was no sorcerer named don Juan; Castaneda made it all up. It wasn't even good fiction, some said; both the story and chronology were contradictory. It certainly wasn't science, backed up with field notes and cross references. Many thought the University of California, Los Angeles (UCLA) was wrong to give him a PhD.

More turned on by the controversy than irritated by it, I decided to ignore the critical issues and confusing biographical anecdotes and just enjoy the strange urgency of Castaneda's retellings of his adventures in book after book. By the 1980s, I was eagerly awaiting every new instalment.

It wasn't just the fascinating stories and shenanigans with the old shaman, or the constant underlying controversy about the author. Fact or fiction, there was always the feeling that a door or window to another world was opening, revealing unexpected, exciting and frightening things that had a strange believability and threatened to leap through the hatch of Castaneda's words into our world. To my disappointment, intervals between books became longer. While his first five action-packed books were published in less than ten years, it took 20 years for the next six to appear, and they were more reflective and philosophical.

Castaneda's first four books narrated his adventures as a sorcerers' apprentice, wandering the deserts, mountains, towns and cities of central and northern Mexico with his teachers. His next four books told of his struggle to understand and come to terms with what he'd been taught after his teachers had gone.

Then, in 1993 a new kind of Castaneda book arrived on the stands, *The Art of Dreaming*. It had strange and discordant elements, including a change of tone that seemed to indicate a ghost-writer was involved. (No pun intended.) The adventures were even more outlandish, with some unbelievable plot turns.

Castaneda abruptly introduced several new characters. They apparently were contemporaries from UCLA. Three women suddenly materialized retroactively in the Mexican desert with important roles in the story. Two of them had written their own books, paralleling Castaneda's work. Their eponymous main characters met and interacted with Castaneda and his by-now legendary sorcerer teachers. The reader had to accept these new authors as equals alongside Castaneda and the original group of apprentices.

In 1998 and 1999, five years later, two final books appeared. One was yet another new kind of work, containing a collection of exercises, *Magical Passes*, which supposedly also derived from ancient Mexican shamanic tradition. Castaneda had moved to Los Angeles, in the "real" world, and was no longer an apprentice. Now, he was a leader. His followers, sometimes called 'disciples', were led by the three women who had been abruptly inserted into the story earlier.

Castaneda was reported to be old and ailing while surrounded by intrigue among his followers as to who was in, who was out, who was high in the hierarchy, and who was just a hanger-on. There was an unspoken concern about who would inherit his enterprise that had sold many millions of books in numerous languages, (and continues to do so). Some months after, I read that Carlos Castaneda died in secret while the three women, his new co-sorcerers, mysteriously disappeared. They have never been seen again.

A final book was published posthumously the next year, 1999, *The Active Side of Infinity*. It read like a nostalgic and self-congratulatory retelling of events from Castaneda's early life. He grew up with his rancher grandfather somewhere in South America, in an adventure-filled childhood that put Huck Finn's to shame. This book gave the impression that it was also composed with a helper, with a female voice, at least at the beginning. But as the narrative built momentum the old author took over. Castaneda delivered several final fables that condensed and summarized the main challenges encountered in his outlandish yet compelling writings. How did he come up with this epic story? And what should we do with it?

In his last chapters ever written, Castaneda introduced a dramatic new and unbelievable actor in his philosophy. The 'flyers' are creatures from the unknown depths of the universe that live with us on earth, unseen. There are millions of them, resembling giant, primitive 'mud shadows' that fly and hop around us all the time. Their constant malevolent presence terrorizes us. Whenever our consciousness rises to a better level they smother us, consuming our emerging awareness, which is their food. The flyers deprive us of our human birthright of magic. They reduce us to our petty, powerless and self-absorbed state.

It's an unexpected and shocking development in the last chapters of his final book. But a vivid description of the flyer appeared in the first book without identification or explanation. To have it reappear three decades later, at the very end, this time with a full introduction and explanation, unexpectedly and provocatively tied up Castaneda's philosophy into a consistent whole.

After the introduction of the flyer, he had one more surprise. Castaneda wrote many stories and recollections over thirty years. All were carefully composed and placed to teach specific points. After twelve books claiming to be authentic histories of lived events, and at the very end of his life, Castaneda ended his long writing career with the story of Antoine.

Antoine was an orphan-child adopted by Castaneda's grandmother on the advice of a sorcerer. Just before her death, she transferred her entire fortune to him. He charmed the old lady with poems, songs and his dazzling personality. As he departed from her and her dispossessed relatives for the last time, he dedicated and recited a beautiful, original poem to her with great drama and romantic flourishes. Grandmother listened, sighed deeply, thanked him profusely and then said:

'Plagiarized, Antoine?'

'Of course, Mother,' he said. 'Of course.'

WHAT GOOD IS Castaneda to us as a writer, as a thinker, and as a person? Hopefully, this book will stimulate curiosity about this question. My analysis is not biographical. I haven't researched Castaneda's life, and I tried not to refer to anything beyond what is inside his books.

New-age seekers, casual readers, and skeptical detractors alike generally read parts of his work up to the fourth or fifth book and then abandoned it, either outraged or confused. More intense followers continued reading until the end of the entire opus, with its more than a million words, when everything abruptly stopped. Castaneda died and his close associates all disappeared together. Many felt he had, almost contemptuously, left behind no believable explanation or plausible way to continue thinking positively about him. Could it be true that Castaneda intentionally misrepresented himself for thirty years and dragged so many other people into his false narrative for so long? And for what purpose?

At this point, it may be fair to say that among both followers and detractors there is a fatigue about the name Castaneda. Few readers want to think about him right now. Many would like to strangle him, like dona Soledad did.

I suspect it would be impossible to understand Castaneda's

work by researching his biographical life, by checking the data and interviewing people who knew him or followed him. But some of us can't just walk away from him, either. Regardless whether what he wrote was fiction or autobiography, no one before him ever reached into the world he explored and brought it forward the way he did. He awakened a consciousness of a part of our past that had not been widely thought of.

Reading Castaneda tends to produce a choice between two reactions: embracing it fully, even to the point of cult-like adoration, or outright rejection. There is a third option.

We can take him at his literary word. At several points of his four decade literary adventure, he admitted he failed to finish his apprenticeship. He ended up, at best, a sorcerer who loved adventures in the unknown as opposed to a seer who sought freedom. And the narrative about Antoine, with its placement at the end of both his final book and his life, strongly hints he wanted to tell us that he judged himself to be a plagiarist. If we consider that to be his death-bed confession and start from there, we can better understand the value of his work and begin to figure out how and why the stories of Carlos Castaneda happened the way they did.

Plagiarism, considered narrowly, means copying someone else's work, word for word, and attributing them to one's self. Considered more broadly, it could mean appropriating the broad outline and meaning of someone else's true or fictional story, and inserting one's self into the narrative. Considered this way, Castaneda's work could have come from an unknown manuscript. It could have come from an original source's oral rendition. Whether manuscript or oral rendition, it could have been the product of an unwritten tradition extending back over generations and centuries.

The works of Homer were not original creations; they were not composed by a man named Homer. They were the final written compilations of a centuries-old oral tradition. The stories were composed before writing was invented and handed down for hundreds of years from storyteller to storyteller. Each generation of storytellers learned techniques of memory which enabled them to maintain the structure and integrity of the work and communicate the essence that there was once a race of great men and women who had heroic adventures.

Before writing was widely adopted, history could be preserved over generations without ever being written down. Once writing came to be used, that type of epic ability to remember disappeared. We don't know what, if anything, really happened on the plains of Troy, but the version recorded in writing 300 years later has been a seminal part of Western civilization. Storytelling may be the highest form of sorcery, connecting our everyday consciousness with a deeper, ancient awareness.

Another way to look at this: consider the recent work of Patrick O'Brian and other authors. O'Brian studied countless diaries, ship-logs and maritime documents from the early 19th century. He then wrote a series of novels with invented characters and imagined events mixed with historical characters and historical events. The result, the highly-regarded series of 20 "Aubrey-Maturin" novels, though clearly fiction, expresses truth that is impossible to convey using proper historical criteria and traditional literary standards.

Perhaps Castaneda did something like that. He may have transcribed some ancient knowledge he became acquainted with into his own modern story. The ancient tradition he refers to is even further lost in time than the story of Troy was to the

Greek storytellers. It's impossible to say if heroes like Achilles and Hector really lived. It's also impossible to confirm the stories Castaneda tells of don Juan and the great sorcerers of ancient Mexico, or the tales of his contemporary cohorts. While they may or may not be true, a great storyteller can convey important historical and religious truths telling stories.

It's not easy to clearly define or even name the ancient religion Castaneda depicts in his books. By the time our current major religions started, its era was already long past. But themes from it still reverberate in many places today. It is the religion whose last remnant believers and practitioners were still sought out and destroyed by the Inquisition of Christianity only several centuries ago.

Belief in this same ancient tradition of magic and witchcraft, though officially banned everywhere now, still persists in almost all non-urban areas in the world. The other night, in Indonesia where I live, my six-week old son, Alex, woke up screaming. We calmed him down from his nightmare – it took several minutes to get him to stop flailing his arms angrily. My Javanese mother-in-law calmly explained that Alex had been "pinched" by his guardian spirit. She says that when infants seem to smile or laugh at a private joke, and when they gaze over your head instead of looking at you, they are watching and reacting to gestures from this spirit.

In our popular culture, new epic legends of magic abound in books and films. Some are placed in an imagined European city or middle earth; some in a galaxy far, far away. With their dimensional scope, intricate plots, and exemplary heroes and villains, these modern epics entertain us by tickling the senses of our ancient heritages, unseen powers, and future possibilities.

Castaneda says that we have a powerful nostalgia for a long-past human era – an era of magic and sorcery that lasted much longer than our current rationalistic period. Humanity may have existed on earth for more than a million years; our current religions only appeared two to five thousand years ago. The co-called "age of reason" only started 200 years ago. Reason has denied and buried the old beliefs, but they are a huge part of our heritage. Our rational consciousness is just the tip of our iceberg. We long for the remainder of ourselves, and for that lost era. There are things we left behind there which are worth rediscovering.

For the most part, modern-day myths that dominate our bookstores and movie theaters don't endeavor to explain how their magic could be possible. They don't bother with metaphysics; they just use magic words or wands. Castaneda labored mightily to explain how and why don Juan's magic worked. He described, in minute detail, an entire universe where magic is possible. He told us how it used to be, and could still be, and dared us to prove or disprove it.

3

POWER PLANTS

I *n the summer of 1960, while I was an anthropology student at* *UCLA, I made several trips to the Southwest to collect infor-* *mation on the medicinal plants used by the Indians of the* *area. The events I describe here began during one of my trips.'*

THESE MEMORABLE OPENING lines of his first book, *The Teachings of Don Juan: A Yaqui Way of Knowledge,* published in 1968, describe the beginnings of Castaneda's remarkable journey which eventually resulted in international fame and infamy, along with another eleven highly popular and controversial books.

For many of us in America, 1968 was the ultimate year of the sixties decade. Many of the tumultuous social movements of that decade seemed to peak that year: President Johnson withdrew from politics; civil rights leader Martin Luther King and Senator Robert Kennedy were assassinated; Richard Nixon was elected President. It was the worst year of the Vietnam War, with more than 1,400 Americans dying every month on average. Hippies grooved and students protested. On Christmas Eve, men went to the moon for the first time, and would land on the moon the next summer.

During this turbulent year, Carlos Castaneda appeared unexpectedly on the scene. *The Teachings of Don Juan* was published, and told the story of a UCLA grad student who had a five-year apprenticeship with an Indian sorcerer in Mexico. The idea of that happening in the same era men were going to the moon exploded into the media. Excerpts from reviews and blurbs on covers of subsequent paperbacks described it as 'a journey into the heart of magic with Carlos Castaneda'. A comment from *The New York Times* said: 'One can't exaggerate the significance of what Castaneda has done'.

In the acknowledgements section of the book, six professors from the UCLA were named and thanked for their inspiration, assistance and criticism. Another professor from UCLA wrote the foreword and hailed the book as addressing the central issue of anthropology: the entry into other perceptual worlds in order to understand 'that our own world is also a cultural construct'.

CASTANEDA IMMEDIATELY INTRODUCED his readers to one of the most unforgettable characters in what was beginning to be called "new- age" American literature: the awesome sorcerer Juan Matus, simply referred to as don Juan. Castaneda described meeting don Juan Matus at a bus station in 1960 in the border town of Nogales, Arizona.

Juan Matus always downplayed the importance of his personal background and biographical details, but we learned that he was born in 1891 in Arizona. Both of his parents were Yaqui Indians. The Yaquis, originally from Sonora, Mexico, were persecuted and oppressed, almost to the point of extermination in the 19th century during the resistance to Spanish domination and the campaigns for Mexican national unification. These struggles forced many Yaquis to move back and forth between northern Mexico and Arizona. Matus says the Yaquis were treated roughly by both the American and Mexican governments, as well as by other indigenous groups and 'Yoris' (mixed-race Mexicans) in general.

According to Castaneda, in the early 20th century the Yaquis, already diminished in numbers and political power, were again forcibly evicted from their homelands by the Mexican government and made to migrate to southern Mexico. Juan Matus was caught up in this exodus, and as a young child he lost both parents, who died during the forced migration. He ended up working in central Mexico as a plantation laborer, until his path crossed with Julian Osorio, a former actor turned sorcerer who drew Matus into his sorcery group.

Since Matus was Yaqui, and Castaneda interacted with him mainly in the Sonoran desert, their homeland, he assumed that Yaqui culture and history shaped don Juan's teachings, and even subtitled his first book *A Yaqui Way of Knowledge*. Only later he learned that Matus' practices and teachings did not come from a Yaqui heritage, but from central Mexico. Some of his cohorts were Yaquis, but many were from other Mexican groups, and some were Europeans. One sorcerer predecessor in his group was Chinese. Castaneda himself was an American citizen, originally from Peru or Argentina.

By the time Matus crossed paths with Castaneda, almost 50 years later, he was turning 70. His grandson Lucio, who, like most Yaquis, disapproved of sorcery and peyote, had been told that his grandfather had 'used to run with' a powerful group of sorcerers, but then became reclusive and obsessed with peyote and esoteric knowledge. But Lucio was proud that his grandfather, at an advanced age, was still as agile and strong as a young man, and 'impossible to sneak up on'.

CASTANEDA RETOLD the story of his first meeting with don Juan at the Nogales bus station several times in later books. Each time he added more detail and depth. In his first book, he described their meeting in just three paragraphs. Castaneda said he talked aimlessly, pretending to be a researcher who knew about local flora and fauna and the culture of the native Americans in the area. Matus sat silently and fixed him with an unforgettable stare, seemingly unimpressed. Then, the old man abruptly and rudely stood up and got on a bus, though he did offer to meet again.

In his 1971 book, *A Separate Reality*, he took three pages for the same story. He talked about how he and his guide, Bill, looked several times for a man Bill described as an eccentric dealer in medicinal herbs before finding him unintentionally at the bus station. This time around, Castaneda remembered that Matus' eyes shined 'with a light of their own' and that he had to avoid his gaze.

In his final book, *The Active Side of Infinity*, 39 years after their first meeting, he devoted two chapters delving into it. He described his and Bill's eventful search for Juan Matus, driving through the desert, hearing Bill's stories of his lifelong interest and association with the native groups of the area. Castaneda realized that Bill was dying and making his final visits to say goodbye to old friends. Castaneda remembered coming upon don Juan abruptly, and talking and acting as if not of his own volition. He said that don Juan somehow paralyzed him with his eyes, to make him stop talking and even thinking. A bus showed up seemingly out of nowhere, and the old man mysteriously covered the 50 yards to the door of the bus in a few effortless leaps.

In this last retelling, Castaneda went to Yuma, Arizona, at Bill's urging, where he got information where to find the old man again. He devoted an additional full chapter telling a long story of his next trip to Mexico when he had to enlist two local conmen, Jorge Campos and Lucas Coronado, to help him locate the old sorcerer. This effort took most of a year, multiple trips to Mexico, and some small and large bribes that all led to a dead end. At that point, as if by accident, they located Matus' son and then Matus himself.

Having finally found Juan Matus, Castaneda spent five years commuting between Los Angeles and Mexico from 1961 to 1965. He dedicated himself to writing notes and learning all he could, with hopes of earning both literary fame and his PhD at UCLA. His relationship with the old man gradually changed from student to apprentice. Instead of simply reporting on the old sorcerer and his knowledge of plants, he joined in with don Juan and his cohorts as they ate or smoked the plants. This continued until 1965, when Castaneda became fearful and confused about his experiences with don Juan's 'power plants' and withdrew from the apprenticeship. He returned to Los Angeles, continued his studies and wrote his first book, which took three years to compose from his field notes and memories.

THE TEACHINGS *of Don Juan* describes Castaneda's experiences with three types of natural hallucinogenic plants found in the deserts of Mexico: peyote, datura and mushrooms. Don Juan referred to them as 'power plants'. Native Americans knew of these plants for thousands of years, and used them for medicinal and religious purposes. Elaborate rituals for collecting, cultivating and preparing them had been developed and passed down.

The planting, harvesting, preparation and consumption of each plant involved numerous detailed procedures and meticulous planning over several years. Many readers in the 1960s and later were thrilled to learn that these 'power plants' had been cultivated and used as part of an ancient, indigenous American culture. According to Castaneda, there were still sorcerers living this life out in the deserts of the southwest US and Mexico.

Collecting peyote with Matus involved trekking for several days to isolated locations in the Mexican deserts to find undisturbed plants. The top parts of the plant were harvested in a ritualistic way using a special knife. Attending to the damage caused to the plant was important. Castaneda was taught that to maximize the plant's benefits, and to ensure his own safety as a participant, he had to treat the plant with utmost respect.

Using peyote meant eating the material of the plant, either in one-on-one sessions supervised by Matus or during overnight vigils with a group of other participants. Castaneda drove for hours sitting in the back of pickup trucks over rocky roads to remote mountain locations, then joined peyote-eating ceremonies, called *mitotes*, where groups of Mexicans sat in a circle chanting.

In one of the mitotes, a local dog got caught up in the ritual. An inspired Castaneda saw the dog as an iridescent, transparent being. He ran and played with it. He could read the being's thoughts, and knew the wondrous creature also read his. The next day, the bemused owner said he watched Castaneda wrestle with his dog, and that the animal peed on him.

In the 1960s, most Mexicans considered themselves to be sophisticated and modern, and resented being seen as primitive by visitors from the north. Most of them had turned against the old traditions that the culture of peyote had grown out of. Nevertheless, Matus attempted to convince his teenage grandson, Lucio, to get serious about his life by taking peyote under his grandfather's guidance. Lucio was disgusted and embarrassed by the idea initially, but finally relented and offered to do it if the American visitor (Castaneda) would buy him a motorcycle. Matus and Castaneda showed up with the peyote, but a group of friends also arrived with some tequila and a record player. Modernity prevailed: they listened to loud music and drank shots instead.

The outcome of a peyote-eating ritual centered on having an encounter with an anthropomorphic figure named Mescalito. It was important to approach Mescalito with the proper attitude. If Mescalito accepted a supplicant, he would teach him the proper way to live. He 'shows things and tells what is what'.

Mescalito was playful instead of frightful and threatening with Castaneda. Matus said he had never seen Mescalito play with anyone before, and regarded that as a command for Matus to take Castaneda as his apprentice and teach him everything he knew, to pass on his knowledge.

THE SECOND POWER PLANT, datura, also known as the 'devil's weed', had to be planted and cultivated personally. Unlike peyote, which is a teacher, the devil's weed was purely a source of power. If not used carefully and correctly, the user could become deranged or injured by it.

Castaneda had to plant and care for his own datura bush, which happened in a secret location over several years. Once matured, it was dug up, and the stem, roots, leaves, flowers and seeds were separated. All these prepared ingredients were stored in a ritualistic way for another year before they could be used.

The roots contained the plant's power boost. An extract made from the root was drunk on repeated occasions until the power was tamed. Taming the power qualified a man to prescribe it to others, to give them a temporary boost of virility for their personal quests, or for their lives and relationships. The stem and leaves could be prescribed to cure diseases; the flowers could be used to control or influence people.

Further preparation of devil's weed involved mashing the plant material with bugs, beetles and a few drops of blood, and then boiling that mixture into extracts. Datura had some strange usages, like being made into a paste to rub on the eyes of lizards, enabling them to act as spies and messengers.

This plant liked men and women of strong and violent character, infusing them with even more power. Matus became concerned that Castaneda enjoyed the devil's weed too much. Matus himself had long decided he didn't like its effect.

'There is no use for it any more. In other times, like those my benefactor told me about, there was reason to seek power. Men performed phenomenal deeds, were admired for their strength and feared and respected for their knowledge. My benefactor told me stories of truly phenomenal deeds that were performed long, long ago. But now we, the Indians, do not seek that power any more. Nowadays, the Indians use the weed to rub themselves, to cure their boils ... It was different when there were people in the world, people who knew a man could become a mountain lion, or a bird, or that a man could simply fly. So I don't use the devil's weed any more. For what? To frighten the Indians?'

MATUS TAUGHT Castaneda about the third power plant, a mushroom used to make a smoking mixture which he called 'the smoke of diviners'. According to Matus, the smoke is the most complete and marvelous helper a man could have, but also the most dangerous. The user's states of mind before, during and after using the smoke are crucial; it takes a lifetime to become proficient using it.

Preparing a small amount of the mixture as a beginner involved harvesting a species of tiny mushrooms, then storing them in a gourd for a year. Other ingredients were also dried for the same amount of time, then mashed with the mushrooms and smoked in a pipe which had been handed down from shaman to shaman for generations. Precise rituals were not as crucial when using the smoke; the user's state of mind and his intent were of paramount importance.

'It will set you free to see anything you want to see. Properly speaking, it is a matchless ally. But whoever seeks it must have an intent and a will beyond reproach. He needs them because he has to intend and will his return, or the smoke will not let him come back. Second, he must intend and will to remember whatever the smoke allowed him to see, otherwise it will be nothing more than a piece of fog in his mind.'

A CUMULATIVE BARRAGE of frightening psychedelic experiences took a toll on Castaneda. In one session with the smoke, he lost the feeling of having a physical body and experienced himself walking through walls and furniture. A day later, sobered up after sleeping it off, he was confused, and queried Matus about the reality of his experience. He wanted don Juan to reassure him that his smoke-induced experiences were only hallucinations, meant perhaps for teaching purposes, but not real and enduring.

Matus insisted that everything was real, and asserted the seriousness of using the power plants, which didn't cause hallucinations but just revealed what was there. Seeking power with power plants required the user to change his life. Castaneda wouldn't have survived several of his experiences without Matus' expert supervision and protection.

During Castaneda's final peyote session, Mescalito appeared again and offered to answer any important question from Castaneda regarding his life. Castaneda asked Mescalito 'what was amiss' about his life.

The next thing he knew, he found himself separated from the group, alone in the desert. A night of terror followed, with

Castaneda crouching behind a rock, hiding from a monstrous pursuer:

'The noises became gigantic steps. Something enormous was breathing and moving around me. I believed it was hunting for me. I ran and hid under a boulder, and tried to determine from there what was following me. At one moment I crept out of my hiding place to look, and whoever was my pursuer came upon me. It was like sea kelp. It threw itself on me. I thought its weight was going to crush me, but I found myself inside a pipe or a cavity ... I saw huge drops of liquid falling from the kelp. I "knew" it was secreting digestive acid in order to dissolve me.'

THIS FIRST VISION of the flyer was placed here as the answer to Castaneda's query about why his life was 'amiss.' It was left unexplained, and would not be repeated and explained until 30 years later, when the flyer reappeared at the end of Castaneda's last book.

Castaneda withdrew from his apprenticeship with Matus before completing his learning in 1965. After all his experiences, he feared he was irrevocably losing his mind and his ability to function in the normal world.

He returned to UCLA and took three years to recover and write his book, including a 'structural analysis' of his experience written in torturous academic jargon. Later, he would remember: 'I had begun to lose the certainty, which all of us have, that the reality of everyday life is something we can take for granted.'

IN THE TOTAL scheme of Castaneda's writings, his initial experiences using power plants have little importance. Being a member of the 1960's cohort, though, Castaneda originally went out of his way to focus on the psychedelic aspect of his narrative. He filled his first two books mostly with these accounts, and it was these stories that brought him wealth and wide fame. That initial fame placed Castaneda's work incorrectly in the tradition of new-age psychedelicists, who wrote endlessly about using powerful plants, herbs, and drugs to open their minds to wondrous new realities and Eastern religious truths.

By the end of the second book, Castaneda realized that the power plants were not that important to don Juan. He only used them as a short-term tool to shock apprentices out of their lethargy. They didn't lead Castaneda into new-age visions of strawberry fields with rainbows and white rabbits, but into a darker world with a frightening ancient feeling to it. Fearful powers hovered there, which stalked and dominated all but the most sober and responsible visitors.

4

EMANATIONS OF INTENT

What was it about power plants that made them so effective in opening Castaneda's awareness and breaking down his defences? According to Matus, every sentient being in our world, including plants, has an unseen cocoon of energy, which interacts with the energy-at-large from the universe.

Generally the cocoons of living beings are similar in proportion to their physical bodies. The cocoon of a large tree is slightly larger than the physical tree. The cocoon of a man or woman is the size of the person with his or her arms and legs extended. The cocoon of most small plants is similar in size to the physical plant.

The cocoons of power plants are unusual. Even though physically they can be tiny plants, they have cocoons 'almost as big as a man's body and three times its width'. The cocoons of power plants have many characteristics in common with humans, but with a wider range of energetic connection to the universe. Power plants also have characteristics that give them a special ability to 'break the barrier of perception'.

To understand what this means, and to follow Castaneda's journey further into his post-psychedelic apprenticeship, we need to leap forward and explore the basic elements and terminology of don Juan Matus' world view. The concepts that drive Castaneda's onward learning are all developed in his later books, but we need them to understand events described in the early books as well.

Usually, when we try to explain life on earth and human awareness from a rational or scientific point of view we imagine them evolving from a primitive state to a more complex state. We start by postulating two separate elements: matter and energy. Over eons of time, we assume that matter and energy interacted and combined until a critical mass was reached. Then, some kind of random spark happened which caused life to emerge from the primordial swamp. Unintelligent life developed and evolved over further eons until another critical mass was reached and another random spark made awareness and intelligence appear, as if out of nowhere.

Castaneda's view is that life and awareness are inherently intertwined, pre-existing and eternal. At its most basic level, and from and to eternity, the universe consists of strands of luminous energy that are already alive and aware. Life with awareness does not evolve from a lifeless condition. It exists everywhere and manifests repeatedly in a multitude of different forms.

It's nearly impossible to describe these strands of aware energy because we are made of them. By projecting our limited imagination onto them, we can visualize them as filaments or emanations. We can't say if they're large or small. Each one stretches endlessly into an infinite length and eternity unto itself. Billions of them can pass through our being.

This energy is aware and conscious of itself, sizzling, alive and moving with the universe's momentum and purpose. These strands can be called the universe's commands, or its intention. They are infinite strings of indescribable energetic awareness.

'As I stared at the wondrous sight, filaments of light began to radiate from everything on that prairie. At first it was like the explosion of an infinite number of short fibers, then the fibers became long threadlike strands of luminosity bundled together into beams of vibrating light that reached infinity. There was really no way for me to make sense of what I was seeing, or to describe it, except as filaments of vibrating light. The filaments were not intermingled or entwined. Although they sprang, and continued to spring, in every direction, each one was separate, and yet all of them were inextricably bundled together.'

THESE BASIC ELEMENTS of the universe are infinite. Each is individual and independent, yet they are bundled together to make streams and currents. Together, these infinite numbers of infinite strands make up a vast sea of awareness, with tiny wisps of spray, powerful currents and unknown depths.

Life and awareness do not arise from a mass of primordial inert matter and unconscious energy accidentally combining and then evolving randomly. The universe is aware energy and has an uncountable number of moulds, or archetypes, for every kind of sentient being. It somehow casts or stamps us into human form. Our form, then, is a receptacle that interacts with the filaments of universal aware power to perform a magical act: perception.

We materialize and appear as tiny bubbles floating in the immense ocean of indescribable awareness far beyond our understanding. Our existence is an infinitesimally small part of a process wherein this ocean of awareness organizes and knows itself. Our form of life and awareness is only one aspect of an immeasurable universal awareness that has its own intent, a swirling ocean impossible to conceive of or understand.

The universe is basically predatory in nature. Multitudes of entities exist in the universe, preying on each other, seeking each other's awareness. We are at the mercy of vast currents of energy which have awareness, that manifest in many forms. Life forms are born and die constantly. Sentient beings are lent awareness, and the purpose of life is to enrich that awareness and then return it to the endower in an enhanced form.

The universe is predatory because the interaction between life and death is the necessary cause of enhanced awareness. Once a sentient being is born, it enters a dance with death. The constant presence of death, and the awareness of death, causes the enhancement of the individual's and the universe's awareness.

Our position as miniscule outposts of a limited awareness in this vast unknown is precarious. The only possible control we have is the ability to know things within our own small field of energy. Our conscious being is made up of the things which we are given as known; we are like tiny islands floating in a boundless space of unknown powers. We build and maintain our island by learning to perceive selected items. To survive we must protect our island by controlling our own awareness, nourishing our perception of things we know, blocking out the unknown which would otherwise engulf us.

Many types of individual sentient beings exist in the

universe of energetic awareness, including organic beings as well as inorganic entities which have awareness but no bodies. There are hierarchies of awareness. We are aware of many beings that have little or no awareness that we exist and perceive them, such as many insects and microscopic creatures. Entities exist which are aware of us while we are not aware of them, even while we share the same space.

EACH INDIVIDUAL SENTIENT BEING, whether it has an organism or not, has a cocoon made of energy. An individual human is a spherical cocoon the size of the human body with arms and legs extended.

Universal filaments of energy come from infinity to pass through the cocoon's skin, through the inside of the cocoon and out the other side, and onward to the universe again to infinity. The cocoon defines and encloses filaments that pass through itself and then extend outward to infinity in countless directions.

The energy inside and outside of the cocoons is the same; they are the same strands. Humans are made by and directly connected to universal strands of energy that extend out to infinity in all directions.

Certain bundles of universal energy filaments pass through our cocoon. The same grouping of filaments passes through the cocoons of all humans. There is no way to understand how this grouping of incomprehensible strands of aware energy happens, but according to Castaneda the sorcerers and seers of don Juan's ancient tradition can see it directly.

Our earth is also a living and sentient being with a cocoon

that we live inside. Our story is part of the earth's story. The infinite universal filaments that pass through us comprise a small part of the earth's collection of infinite filaments. The lives of our human cocoons take place inside the earth's much larger cocoon, and our fates are linked and intertwined.

Every living being's cocoon contains universal strands of awareness that it uses for perception. Each cocoon is filled with billions of universal strings of aware energy, which comprise only an infinitesimally small part of the total strings of the entire universe. A single cocoon, though small in comparison to the whole, still contains countless billions of strings of aware energy inside itself.

Only a small portion of those enclosed strings are used. Every living being has a feature in its cocoon which selects some emanations to use for perception while disregarding others. This feature is the point where every sentient being is connected to the universe, directly connected to the spirit and intention of the universe.

Humans have an orb of bright energy about the size of a tennis ball located on the surface of the cocoon, about an arm's length behind the right shoulder. This ball of energy is the agent which selects emanations passing through our cocoons to use for perception. It's called the assemblage point because it's the point where perception is assembled.

Only a small portion of the total number of emanations inside the cocoon is selected, while the rest are ignored. If the assemblage point moves around on the surface or the inside of the cocoon it selects whatever encased universal emanations it falls on. Those internal strands of awareness are then connected to the same strands outside the cocoon stretching to infinity, and this is how perception occurs.

Perception is a magical process that happens when strands of universal energy passing through our human cocoons are selected and then lit up by our assemblage point. The assemblage point connects, aligns and lights up the internal and external parts of those selected strings of energy which extend out to infinity. The result is perception. We learn where to place our assemblage point and, therefore, what to perceive, from our parents and caretakers, starting from the moment of birth.

We can say a human being has an assemblage point. It may be more correct to say that the universe has untold trillions of assemblage points. We are what we are, and live in our world because of the position of our assemblage point in the universe of aware energy.

The assemblage point exists inside a cocoon, in a universe of aware energy. By selecting and combining strands of aware emanations, an assemblage point simultaneously assembles a world and also an aware being in that world. The particular nature of that world and of that being is determined by the selection of energy strands and the degree and intensity of awareness. The intention that makes the assemblage point assemble perception comes from the universe outside the cocoon.

According to Castaneda, the total energy inside our cocoons is divided into two parts. One part is the human band, which is the collection of energy accessible to human perception, made up of about one-third of the entire cocoon. The other two-thirds are non-human strands of energy inside our cocoons but outside the human range of perception.

The human band is organized in 48 bundles. To perceive our normal world, we use two of these bundles. There are 46 additional bundles of energy inside our cocoons which we can learn to use but don't normally use. Of those 46 bundles, six belong to a twin realm of beings which also live with us on earth. They also have cocoons and assemblage points, but they don't have physical organisms which breathe, eat and reproduce.

Many of these beings who exist with us are aware of us, but we are not normally aware of them. Don Juan Matus sometimes referred to them as our 'twins', sometimes as our 'cousins'. They are aware of us, but cannot contact us. We are usually not aware of them, but if we do become aware of them we can take the initiative and contact them, which can then open the door to relationship.

The number and variety of these twin entities which share our daily world, but outside our normal awareness, are greater than the number and variety of entities we normally perceive throughout our lives. The variety of unseen and nonorganic entities in our world far exceeds the thousands of organic species we have counted so far.

The other 40 bundles of energy in the human band of our luminous spheres belong to other worlds. If we used all of them it would be possible to assemble at least 600 additional complete worlds. More than 600 worlds are available to us, using the energy that passes through the human band in our luminous spheres.

These worlds are as complete and engulfing as ours; beings live and die in them, and we can visit them and live and die in them, too. If one were to ask where in the universe these worlds exist, it's impossible to say, other than to say that these worlds, and the beings that live or visit there, exist in their respective positions of assemblage.

They exist constantly and independently of our world, but

are inaccessible to us. We're protected from them because we're conditioned to ignore them and to assume that our normal world of everyday life is the only possible reality. If our assemblage point stays rigid in one place, there is a wall of perception between us and the twin occupants of our world, and between our world and any other world.

There are untold trillions of positions in the universe where assemblage points can assemble worlds and beings. All living beings have cocoons and assemblage points in the flow of the universe's string-like emanations of aware energy.

The cocoon is a temporary feature, starting at birth and ending at death. Castaneda doesn't explain how the birth of a cocoon occurs in this universe of aware energy. He says that every sexual act causes feelings and other constituent parts which normally float undisturbed in the universe to try to combine and cause a new being to be conceived. Death happens when the cocoon weakens from usage and collapses, allowing the enclosed energy to escape back into the universe at large.

Cocoons exist in a constantly moving ocean of universal power. This power, which contains the universe's awareness and its intent, rolls onto the cocoons constantly. This 'rolling force' has two aspects to it. The first is what gives us life, purpose and awareness; the second is the power that breaks open and destroys the cocoon at the moment of death. This dual force of life and death strikes us constantly throughout our lifespan, gradually wearing out the cocoon until it can no longer use the rolling power but instead is overcome by it.

The aware energy trapped inside the cocoon constantly moves and struggles to connect with the energy outside. The endless strands on the outside exert constant pressure on the cocoons. The outside pressure initiates consciousness by stopping the movement of the trapped energy, which is always fighting to get out – in effect, fighting to die. When the emanations inside connect with the emanations outside, awareness begins and death is forestalled. We must perceive or die.

Our perception always involves the totality of our energy. There is no extra energy inside our cocoons that is not involved in the act of perception, of being in our world.

We are perceivers. That is what we are born to do. In an infinite predatory universe that is far beyond our comprehension, we have a safe island of all we are given as known as our haven. Other unknown types of sentient life exist around us, and some of them are aware of us, but our wall of perception hides them from us during life. Managing our tiny island, keeping ourselves safe in this vast sea of awareness, takes all our energy, which is the same as saying all of our awareness.

5

WITH THE DONS IN THE DESERT

'I 'm only a man, don Juan,' pleaded Castaneda.

He was responding to Matus' question: 'Do you know anything about the world around you?'

In 1968, Castaneda returned to Mexico and restarted his apprenticeship with don Juan Matus. This launched the final phase of their relationship, which continued uninterrupted until Matus' disappearance in 1973.

The above exchange epitomized the banter between Castaneda and his teacher as they roamed the deserts and towns. Don Juan would put his hat on, throw it on the ground, slap his thigh, flash a piercing or quizzical stare, crack a joke, crack his joints, open his eyes wide, pat Castaneda on the back, and smack his lips. Curious, perplexed, annoyed, frightened and exasperated, Castaneda would ask questions constantly, usually unnecessarily. If Castaneda's writing is all fantasy, then his literary ability to depict a sorcery apprentice's prideful yet fearful and halting progress from ignorance to understanding is masterful. Castaneda the apprentice always understood and misunderstood just the right amount at every instance, and showed it with his evasions, denials, obsessive tics and other reactions.

Don Juan's sidekick was introduced: the fearful yet comical, acrobatic sorcerer, don Genaro Flores. He became the assistant teacher in Castaneda's new, sometimes slapstick, apprenticeship. Don Genaro, a Mazatec Indian from central Mexico, appeared as a simple country peasant, shy and self-deprecating. He continually amused, provoked and terrified Castaneda with inexplicable and sophisticated acts of magic mixed with theatricality and pantomime.

Along with don Genaro, Matus also introduced Nestor and Pablito, his other apprentices. They would accompany Castaneda on most of his exploits from this point onward. Castaneda's scary apprenticeship was infused with humor from then on, with Latino macho comradery to the point of jokes about farts and women's underwear. Don Juan said he wanted to lighten things up; he said Castaneda's earlier withdrawal had been caused by taking things too seriously.

Castaneda still tried to take notes surreptitiously, and got teased endlessly for it; don Genaro ridiculed him for always having his hands in his pockets, where he kept his notebooks. Genaro stood on his head to show the absurdity of trying to become a sorcerer by taking notes.

Castaneda fearfully told don Juan he didn't want any more peyote. He didn't want his sense of reality overturned by Matus' teachings again. He just published a successful and critically acknowledged best-seller, and was planning lucrative lecture tours like the one I just missed, and was closing in on his PhD. An internationally famous, successful man is normally not a candidate for a sorcery apprenticeship operated out of a ramshackle shack in the Mexican desert. Matus just ignored this, and welcomed Castaneda back like a prodigal son to continue his learning. Without knowing why, Castaneda followed along.

MANY READERS of Castaneda were excited by the psychedelic adventures of the first two books, but then lost interest gong forward as they realized that hallucinogenic plants no longer were involved. In fact, by the end of the events in his second book, *A Separate Reality*, Castaneda stopped using all forms of power plants. He had used peyote, devil's weed and the mushroom smoking mixture from 1960 to 1965, as described in the first book. But by the time he returned to Mexico in 1968, the stock of plants and mushrooms he cultivated earlier and then abandoned had died off or decomposed. From 1968 to 1969, he reported few instances when he smoked the mushroom mixture, but only because Matus insisted. He had to use Matus' stash as he had none of his own.

Matus explained that the plants were necessary to shake Castaneda out of a lethargic condition, although at significant cost to his body. He needed to be shocked into the realization that there are other states of consciousness and other worlds. To realize this, he had to have his shields broken down.

Our shields are composed of our internal and external dialog – our habitual and obsessive way of thinking and projecting our thoughts onto perception without pause. Shields are both the cause and effect of our assemblage point being held rigidly in one place. We were taught how to immobilize and stabilize our perception through our habitual talking and thinking; our talking and thinking processes then became our shields.

In his second, third, and fourth books Castaneda described a series of learning experiences evolving in a pattern. Don Juan would manoeuvre Castaneda into a position to confront a possibly dangerous learning challenge. Castaneda would sense this and become nervous and fidgety, asking questions, seeking reassurance or directions, trying to change the subject or find the brake pedal. Finally, Matus would abruptly push him into whatever challenge had materialized. Castaneda would then fall into it haphazardly. He would misidentify opportunities and dangers, then invariably fall helplessly into a trap or peril by overindulging in his emotional reactions.

Castaneda encountered a 'guardian of the other world', manifested as a giant gnat. He saw this guardian several times until one encounter turned dangerous. The guardian gave him a signal to go away: he mooned Castaneda, showing his backside. It had multi-colored designs on it and Castaneda was awed and stared at it. The monster was offended and attacked; Castaneda only survived because of don Juan's intervention.

Another time, Castaneda gazed dreamily at the water in an irrigation stream, ignoring don Juan's warnings and instructions, and was transported away by the water. He found himself too far away, lost in an unknown realm, with no idea where he was or how to return. Matus again rescued him, but this experience made all bodies of water dangerous for him; he couldn't be left alone anywhere near water for a time.

Castaneda had lost some of the shields which formerly made his wall of perception to protect himself. He wasn't ready, though, to take responsibility for his encounters in the separate reality he now encountered. He failed to identify opportunity and respect danger, or to remove himself from harm. He would only indulge in whatever came along, as if he didn't believe it was really happening, or as if he was simply studying some interesting phenomenon, or day-dreaming.

A dangerous world of power continued to open. Matus was repeatedly forced to rescue Castaneda at the end of each experience. He needed supervision and protection to prevent him from wandering too far and being lost forever in a different world, or from being injured or even killed in a thoughtless encounter with a larger power that he didn't acknowledge or respect.

The real danger, and the real adventure, began once don Juan stopped giving Castaneda power plants. The events in his apprenticeship began to have a different impact and value, and marked a new phase of his entire life. Once his apprenticeship continued without eating peyote or smoking mushrooms, he could no longer call his experiences hallucinations. Everything was equally real and equally important.

If he was eating peyote or mushrooms, or using the smoke, Castaneda could attribute any extreme experiences or frightening encounters to the power plants, not to himself as perceiver, or the actual world at large. Once Castaneda realized that other realities existed and impacted on him on their own, everything changed. Matus told him that ...

'The world is indeed full of frightening things and we are helpless creatures surrounded by forces that are inexplicable and unbending. The average man believes those forces can be explained or changed ... sooner or later. By opening himself to knowledge a sorcerer becomes more vulnerable ... by opening himself to knowledge he falls prey to such forces and has only one means of balancing himself ... he must *feel and act like a warrior. Only as a warrior can one survive the path of knowledge.'*

BY REPEATEDLY SHOCKING Castaneda with power plants Matus made him drop his shields. This opened the doors that separated his normal reality from the irreducible universe of aware energy. Even though his reason still held on and prevented him from seeing it, he was vulnerable to the vast ocean of indescribable predatory awareness that is in the universe at large, and within our own cocoons. Once this openness persisted without any excuses provided by power plants, once it was no longer possible to sleep it off, sober up and come back to normal, there came a turning point. Castaneda outgrew the need to be jolted by peyote or mushrooms.

But why would a famous successful man want or allow himself to be open to 'inexplicable and unbending' forces?

According to don Juan Matus, this is the paradox of awareness: to protect ourselves from the inexplicable and unbending forces that are all around us we must control our awareness. But if all we do in life is control our awareness we deprive ourselves of our birthright as humans, as perceivers capable of magic.

During the period of peyote and mushroom usage, while Matus was giving him the power plants to shock him into a new openness, he was also teaching Castaneda techniques that would prepare him to face that insoluble paradox of awareness. He showed him a way of living that allowed perceivers to expand their awareness while protecting themselves from the unrelenting and inexplicable forces that attack any emerging awareness.

Earlier, Castaneda arrogantly ignored those teachings. Now, he needed them to protect his life and sanity. These survival techniques became the topic of the third book, *Journey to Ixtlan*.

Castaneda says this book was based on field notes from his earlier years with Matus; he set them aside because he didn't realize their importance. They are lessons from Matus which, right from the start, taught him how to begin moving through the world like a 'warrior', to tap into new awareness and power while withstanding the assaults of the unknown.

Castaneda was forced to accept that his outlandish experiences were not simply attributable to peyote, and that the challenges he encountered were inescapable parts of being human. Anyone who sought knowledge opened himself to the unknown. He became accessible and vulnerable to the vast powers that assaulted him and all human beings. He literally couldn't survive without becoming and reacting as a warrior who had entered a battle and had to save his own life, constantly.

A warrior in a battle can die at any moment. Therefore, the warrior goes to war with fear while wide awake. He respects his situation, stays alert to everything around him, and has full confidence in himself. He doesn't waste his movements or energy, or indulge in unnecessary or unproductive thoughts. He doesn't rely on others or blame them for his predicament. He doesn't assert his status or identity to exalt or protect himself. He sets aside his sense of self-importance; he is equal to everything and everyone.

He knows that death is nearby, and even if he survives this battle he will still die another day. The awareness of death gives him a measure of freedom and abandon, which adds power and flair to his actions. He embraces a certain mood, and holds himself accountable for every experience and outcome. He takes everything seriously, while laughing at all of it.

The chapter titles of his third book list the main themes in Castaneda's system of survival and wellbeing for a warrior in battle: *Erasing Personal History, Losing Self-Importance, Death is an Advisor, Assuming Responsibility, Becoming a Hunter, Being Inaccessible, Disrupting the Routines of Life, The Last Battle on Earth, Becoming Accessible to Power,* and *The Mood of a Warrior.*

Obviously, our normal lives are not organized in a way to create the mood of a warrior. Instead, we constantly assure ourselves that our world is understandable and safe. If we encounter something we can't understand, we assume it will be sorted out safely at some point. A warrior's mood only applies when someone is exposed to extreme and unrelenting danger. Why would anyone in a comfortable life seek to acquire this state of being? Where does the challenge come from that would elicit this mood naturally?

Matus taught Castaneda the art of being accessible or inaccessible, depending on the situation. Just as a man at war could find a place to pause, and thereby gain some ability to choose his next battleground, the man or woman seeking knowledge can learn to be inaccessible or accessible. The warrior can decide consciously when to reveal himself and when to stay hidden from the challenges that are always around him. The warrior chooses to be inaccessible or accessible, instead of helplessly shifting abruptly from a semi-conscious stupor to a frightful awakening.

According to Matus, the natural challenges that will elicit the mood of a warrior are around us all the time. We are literally surrounded by eternity. We keep ourselves inaccessible to it, separate and protected from it. We focus constantly, minute to minute, second to second, on the concerns of our personal lives, which interposes a wall of perception.

Matus endeavored to teach Castaneda the art of being open to the powers that exist all around us without being annihilated by them. He said, 'this world is a mysterious place. To believe that the world is only as you think it is, is stupid.' But to go into the unknown carelessly, in the wrong mood, is even more stupid as it exposes one to dangerous, uncontrollable and unrelenting forces.

He spent days hunting with don Juan in the desert. Matus taught him about the habits of various animals of prey, such as rattlesnakes, small mammals, and birds. Castaneda recalled one late afternoon when he was enjoying a feeling of satisfaction after a day wandering the desert. It was getting cold and they were still far from don Juan's house. Abruptly, Matus stood up, sniffed the air and announced that they were going to climb a nearby hill and stand at the top in a clearing.

As they reached the hilltop, Matus said, 'don't be afraid. I'm your friend and I'll see that nothing bad happens to you.' Of course, these reassuring words had the opposite effect, changing Castaneda's mood to sheer fright.

Matus whispered, 'there it is, look look!' as a gust of wind hit Castaneda in the face.

While Castaneda argued that it was only the wind, which was caused by slight disturbances in air pressure and temperature, Matus asked him to collect some branches from nearby shrubs and bushes. He made Castaneda lie down while he covered them both with the branches and leaves. After lying there quietly for five minutes, the wind died down.

Moments later, after they had sat up and continued their discussion, Matus again pointed out the approach of something, and the wind hit them again. They had to gather new branches and again hide themselves to make it go away.

Matus explained that it was not simply the wind they were confronting at that twilight hour but power itself. The power hid inside the wind, something like a 'whorl, a cloud, a mist, a face that turns around'. The world is truly a mysterious place. Power could be helpful to a hunter or a nuisance. The secret of great hunters is 'to be available and unavailable at the precise turn of the road'.

IN ONE OF the most unforgettable scenes in all of Castaneda's works, don Genaro scaled a cliff and leaped from stone to stone, frolicking on the top of a 150-foot waterfall. He displayed a mastery of balance using fibers from his luminous being to support himself. Castaneda couldn't see the fibers. He could only look. He only perceived a series of impossibly difficult physical movements. He reasoned that it was sleight-of-hand, or possibly that he was hypnotized by the event.

There is a difference between looking and seeing, just as there's a separate reality. We look at one reality but are blind to the separate reality unless we see. Seeing involves using the entire human body, including the unseen parts, as an instrument for perception; seeing happens independently of the eyes.

The overall mood of normal perception dominated by predatory concerns is visual. It has always been of paramount importance for humans to be able to look at a scene, take it in, and quickly recognize both danger and opportunity from a predator's point of view. The eyes learned to look at things, and glance briefly from item to item. The mind learned to fill in the meaning of the scene and each item in it and their values to a predatory being that is both hunting and being hunted.

Looking at things, looking at the world, is a learned behavior. Newborn babies don't look at you. They gaze out and see something else.

'We learn to think about everything, and then we train our eyes to look as we think about the things we look at.'

We learn to think, and in our thoughts we describe the world and our place in it; then we use our thoughts to help our eyes look at things. We beckon known items and our described and specified world into focus. Once we learn that, we look at everything from then on and forget how to see.

According to Matus, normal human vision is 'more interpretation than perception'. We don't bother to use our feel, smell or even our hearing to make complex and binding identifications. Normally, we only 'touch the incoming energy lightly with our eyes', which triggers an interpretation system that immediately identifies and assigns attributes and values: tree, house, woman, old, beautiful, dangerous. Through our strobe-like looking, we make an entire world to live in. We work constantly to maintain and also sharpen our focus on that world, separated from the universe as it was before we learned to filter it through our thoughts and eyes.

We are taught and compelled from infancy to join our group and look at things together; we agree on what is real and what is not. We do this to establish a safe outpost in the unknown, together with all humans who share the same planet. We establish a path to follow throughout life to protect ourselves with our doings from the universal sea of predatory awareness. We separate the known from the unknown, then ignore and deny the unknown.

Castaneda never managed to see, unaided, at any time during his apprenticeship with Matus. It was only later, several years after Matus was gone, that Castaneda's reason relented and allowed him to see. Once he could see, he could also remember everything he had seen before.

By using the power plants Matus impelled Castaneda to open to the powers that exist in the universe. Once he did so, there was no such thing any more as hallucination. Everything, all perception, was equal. There was no more possibility of casually getting high, where he could sleep it off afterwards.

Matus taught Castaneda that there is no casual eating or drinking. There's no casual sex. There is no casual walking in the desert, or city either. In fact, there is no casual thinking. Every thought is an action that controls our awareness and perception, which determines everything. Philosophy is a life and death endeavour. Nothing is real, but everything matters.

MATUS INTRODUCED Castaneda to the topic of dreaming. He said that the safest way to become accessible to the unknown is to develop and utilize a type of awareness we have in our dreams. Men and women are luminous balls of energy living amidst great swirls of energy bands. We perceive ourselves and our world by holding our assemblage point in a specific place, which creates an inner and outer world. The way to access new energy bands, which contain non-ordinary perceptions, is to move the assemblage point. But it cannot be moved by conscious command.

Our assemblage point shifts naturally during sleep, producing our dreams. Exploring our dreams is the easiest way to develop the ability to utilize the movement of the assemblage point. Matus, though, is not talking about analyzing our dreams in a psychoanalytical way. Psychoanalysis of dreams is a way of understanding them according to our existing point of reference, a way of updating or improving our normal perspective and performance by including new information taken from dreams.

Castaneda wrote about developing our attention inside a dream, not looking at it from the outside. As infants, we first assemble our world by focussing our attention exclusively on one position of the assemblage point. He says we can assemble another world by focussing on things that appear in our dreams, when the assemblage point has randomly moved to a different position. In fact, our daily reality is a dream among many dreams, enforced and enhanced because of the agreement of all humans on our planet who share it and renew and enhance it together. The universe is full of dreams with beings sharing them based on their agreements. The universe is filled with assemblage points, places where aware energy is gathered and combined in the act of perception.

It's natural to share dreaming. Our daily reality is just that: a shared human dreaming condition held in unison by many people together. We are unaware that it's a dream because we have no other shared dreams to compare. Our dreamed world is not our arbitrary choice; it came about because it expresses the universe's intent. What we do in it once we find ourselves thrown into a dream is our choice. We must take responsibility for everything that happens, to have any measure of control.

∾

THE FOCUS of Castaneda's work changes in the third book. Instead of being about smoking mushrooms or eating peyote to be jolted out of normal reality, now it is about how we can intentionally move out of our normal reality into another reality without using power plants, and how difficult and dangerous it is to do this. It's a lonely and solitary quest, separating from others in a radical way. Without the precepts of the 'warrior's way', becoming unhinged from accepted reality is simply madness.

During one of his three-day drives from Los Angeles to Mexico, Castaneda spent two nights in a hotel outside a Mexican town while his car was being repaired. From the hotel café he watched a group of poor children who spent their days loitering on the curb outside. They waited patiently for customers to leave, when they would descend on the leftovers and wolf them down, then clean the table and retreat politely again to the curb. Castaneda felt despondent that these children lived with no hope. He offered Matus his judgment that they were deprived of the 'opportunities for personal satisfaction and development' that he himself enjoyed.

'You think that you're better off, don't you?' was Matus' rejoinder. 'Can your freedom and opportunities help you to become a man of knowledge? All the men of knowledge I know were kids like those you saw eating the leftovers and licking the table.'

6

THROWING THE OTHER SELF

OFF A CLIFF

Castaneda recalled a funny day he and Matus spent with don Genaro Flores at his rundown shack in the mountains. The old man delighted them for hours performing hilarious pantomimes and acrobatic gestures, with Castaneda usually as the butt of his jokes. At the end of the afternoon, don Juan excused himself to go to the bushes and urinate.

When Matus returned, Genaro stood up dramatically, sniffed the wind, and said, 'I better go where the wind blows', with an extremely serious expression, then walked off. Matus warned Castaneda not to be worried if he heard strange noises while Genaro was in the bushes, because 'when Genaro shits the mountains tremble'. Minutes later, Castaneda heard a 'deep, unearthly rumble', which he couldn't identify. When he looked at don Juan for a hint what was going on, Matus was doubled over with laughter.

The ultimate aim of Castaneda's guided adventures in the

deserts, mountains and towns of Mexico with his teachers was for him to encounter his 'double', his other self.

According to Castaneda, all humans have another self which exists all the time alongside the self we are normally aware of. Two selves exist because of our two-step process of perception. The other self is a more basic and more complete version of our being than our self of daily life. It needs the daily self to thrive and survive as a predator, and to make sense of life – to have a life, basically. Having awareness of the two selves at the same time is being in touch with 'the totality of ourselves'.

Because of our two-step perception, we always exist as two beings, but we are normally only aware of one. In the act of perception, our core being initially perceives the world directly. We disregard that direct perception, then go a step further to impose our thoughts onto the energy we have just appre-hended. The result of that extra step is the perception of our normal self in our world. We pay attention only to that secondary product of perception.

There is a tiny instant of time between the original direct perception and the secondary one. We use that interval to deny and forget our primary perception and move our full attention to the secondary perception instead. But we still have a self that exists in that first world of perception, even though we deny and disregard it.

Once we learn to do the two steps of perception, which we are taught from the moment of birth, our two selves operate separately. The new self, the self that lives in the agreed-on real world, automatically operates the process of perception throughout life.

'The world doesn't yield to us directly, the description of the world stands in between. So, properly speaking, we are always one step

removed and our experience of the world is always a recollection of the experience. We are perennially recollecting the instant that has just happened, just passed. We recollect, recollect, recollect.'

WE CAN TALK about this process of perception, and the double, and our words can make us feel we have some grasp of the topic, or at least a way to point towards it. But we can't apprehend the double through language. Talking and thinking about the double doesn't put us in touch with it. 'That's the flaw with words. They always make us feel enlightened, but when we turn around to face the world they always fail us and we always end up facing the world as we always have, without enlightenment.'

The other self can be encountered accidentally, due to illness, insanity, love, war or extreme shock. Or it can be encountered more harmoniously but still haphazardly in dreaming. In both cases, our typical reaction is to quickly revert to our world of thinking, which negates the memory of the double or interprets it as something else.

Matus and don Genaro gradually taught Castaneda to encounter his other self, his double, by dreaming it. They went on to guide him to the realization that it's actually the double that dreams the self of normal awareness. This is the mystery of the dreamer and the dreamed.

The dreamer and the dreamed live almost concurrently, separated by a miniscule interval of time. They experience the same events, but perceive them differently. The dreamer's awareness is much more broad and inclusive, while also more disordered and unruly. The dreamer perceives eternity, but cannot speak about it, or about anything.

On the other hand, the awareness of the dreamed self is curtailed, blinkered, organized and protected. The dreamer is aware of the dreamed, but the dreamed has been taught to disregard and deny the dreamer. The dreamer experiences everything immediately, while the dreamed self experiences everything after a time lag. During this microscopic time lag, he imposes his thoughts and images, making the raw data conform to his view of the world.

The dreamed self collects a selection of perceived events during his life and plays them over and over in his mind. He calls this his memory. His personal history and identity are constructed from these selected memories. Most experience is forgotten, but still exists in hidden caches of denied and misunderstood imagery. The paradox of memory is that our memories of the normal self are mostly the denial of memory. To remember in a deeper sense is to remember the other self.

We are taught from birth to focus our attention exclusively on the dreamed self that exists in our shared world into which we have been thrown. We share our world with other beings that are part of our era, our cohort. We have an agreement with them about what is real and what isn't real. According to Matus, to be real means to be agreed upon. This agreement is not self-chosen or arbitrary; it's imposed on us by the universe's intent, for its own purposes which we can't fathom.

Our normal life consists mainly of the constant and engulfing effort to maintain, energize, explain, understand and renew this agreed-on real world. Our deeds, thoughts and words are engaged mainly in the act of asserting the realness of our world that we have been taught since day one.

We are constantly in denial of the double, who is actually the dreamer that dreams us. In this activity, we are accomplishing magic and sorcery. We are denying what is basic and replacing it with a description, a story.

The dreamed person has learned to disregard his other self and its doings. We also disregard our disregarding. We have learned various habitual ways of thinking and doing repetitive and compulsive activities to keep the other self out of awareness. We disregard those efforts, just as we disregard our autonomic body functions which control breathing, digestion, fear. To top it off, we are taught not only to ignore the other self but also to deny it actively, supposedly to simplify our passage through life, to make life easier.

Unless we are taught about it, we are never aware of our double during life until the moment of death. Just before death, when our energy fails and we can no longer perform the two-step process of perception, we lose awareness of our "real" self and revert to our double in whatever condition it may be after a lifetime of neglect. The memories stored then explode into awareness, and we relive them one by one. Our life passes before our eyes.

To teach him about his double self, don Juan and don Genaro continually move Castaneda from his normal self to his double. From the position of their luminous beings, they push the assemblage point on his luminous being. Castaneda experiences this usually as a slap on the back. They often struggle to return him to normal awareness. Sometimes, they can bring him back with another slap on the back, but sometimes it requires throwing buckets of water on him.

The two teachers also continually show Castaneda their

own doubles without telling him what they're doing. The double is not an organism like us that must breathe and eat. Trying to teach while also amusing themselves, they tease and confuse him, daring him to realize he's in the presence of a double that doesn't need to perform normal bodily functions like defecating. The first day Castaneda met don Genaro he met Genaro's double, and it ended in the pretended trip to the bushes described earlier. Castaneda dutifully recorded it in his notes without getting the joke.

A concept like the double can certainly be described as outlandish, even bizarre, but it's actually no weirder than some of the accepted precepts of modern physics. Quantum physics has a very strange concept called superposition, where an electron or other particle can be in two places at once. Superposition also weirdly resembles the double in that it's virtually impossible to observe – when you observe the double particles, the observation collapses and goes back to what is normally conceived, where the particle exists only in one place. According to Castaneda, the double does that too. You can be double, but only one at a time.

THE TOTAL LUMINOUS BEING, which contains both selves, the dreamer and the dreamed, has eight points, which can be visualized.

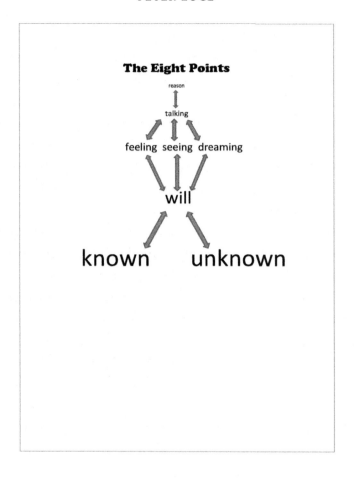

Don Juan drew a diagram in the dust, a geometrical shape with eight points. The eight points, organized from small to large, were called reason, talking, dreaming, seeing, feeling, will, the known, and the unknown.

This diagram had two epicenters: the first epicenter was reason. Don Juan explained that reason dominates our era, even though it is by far the smallest point in the diagram, and it is out on the perimeter and connected to only one other point. Reason is the smallest point, and the most isolated from our total being. We now are living in an age when reason is our epicenter.

The only other point reason connects directly with is called talking. Talking refers to our ongoing internal and external dialog by which we impose our thoughts and learned expectations on the raw data of perception. When reason connects with talking, we call that understanding.

We use only the two smallest points in the totality of ourselves – reason and talking. Normally in our lives we never even become aware of the remaining six points. Reason and talking comprise the normal self of our era in human history.

Talking, though, is connected to three larger points – dreaming, seeing and feeling. Our reason and talking have definitions for those three points, but very constricted definitions. These three concepts also have larger meanings. Dreaming is not simply something done while sleeping, but the movement of the assemblage point with its alignment of new strands of energy, whether done while asleep or awake. Seeing is the initial step of perception, before the interpretation step. It means seeing as opposed to looking. Feeling refers to the feeling of the double, which interacts with the world by projecting tentacles of energy strands outward.

These three points – dreaming, seeing and feeling – do not touch the point of reason; reason cannot connect directly with these three points or anything beyond. These three points and all beyond are unreasonable.

Still, reason is the dominant epicenter in our era. Although the smallest point in the human luminous being, reason is nevertheless something like the hero of modern humanity. Reason rescued us from earlier times when larger, darker powers dominated human life. Reason established its dominion by using language and talking to circumscribe and curtail the meanings of the concepts dreaming, seeing and feeling. Dreaming, seeing and feeling are concepts filled with vast powers, and used to have greater importance in an earlier era of human history when they were dominant, and reason was hardly known at all.

Dreaming, seeing and feeling are connected to a much larger point – will. Will refers to the ability of the luminous being itself to act, with intention, in its own domain where every being appears as a cocoon-like conglomeration of strings of energy that go to infinity. Will acts with its tentacles, its raw strings of aware energy.

From a sorcery point of view, and from ancient man's position, will was the predominant epicenter. Reason was then off to the side, despised and ignored. Will is the central point that organizes the being and the activities of the other self, the dreamer. The world upheld by will is the world of the other self, just as the world upheld by reason is the world of our normal self.

The final two points are the known and the unknown. These points are much larger than the combined total of all the other points. In fact, to put the entire diagram in a more accurate perspective, if we imagined a football stadium, reason would be just the rule book in the referee's pocket, while the known would be the entire stadium, and the unknown would be the infinite world beyond the stadium.

Tales of Power tells the story of Castaneda's final days with don Juan Matus. By the end of the book, Matus and his group of old sorcerers have gone, and Castaneda has leaped off a cliff, along with the other two apprentices, Pablito and Nestor.

To set up the depiction of these events, Castaneda

explained the final two of the eight points on the diagram that makes up the totality of man.

He said that the life of a human being is composed of two sides, which Matus names 'the tonal and the nagual'. These two words are said to come from ancient American folklore; it's hard to find exact English words to replace them. A rough translation of the tonal is 'the known' and the nagual is 'the unknown'.

The known is temporary, beginning at birth and ending at death. The unknown is always there, eternal. The unknown is aware of everything but cannot speak. The known can speak but has a limited controlled awareness; it can point in the general direction of the unknown, if called upon to do so, but is normally not aware of the unknown's existence.

The known goes a step further and actively denies the existence of the unknown. Matus says 'the tonal's great art is to suppress any manifestation of the nagual in such a manner that even if its presence should be the most obvious thing in the world, it is unnoticeable'. We're always surrounded by eternity, but we're busy thinking of important things.

The known is everything we know, or think we know, and everything we have a word for during our lifetime. This includes ourselves as people, our identities, and all the things we identify as being in the world, including God, the soul and the devil and any concept we can think of. The known makes up its own rules by which it apprehends the world and therefore creates and sustains its world. Without the known there would be no meaning, language or order in our perceptions. There would only be indescribable chaos.

The known of any sentient being is best visualized as a small island suspended in a vast universe which is almost completely composed of the unknown. The unknown can be visualized as an entire universe of power and awareness that acts constantly and knows and directs everything, but cannot say anything or understand who it is or what it is doing.

The unknown is everything that exists apart from the tiny island of the known. The unknown is unimaginably immense. When Matus taught his apprentices about this topic, they carried a small table on a four-hour hike into the desert. They found a valley and placed the table on the ground, with kitchen utensils on top. They then hiked for another two hours to the top of a nearby mountain and looked down at the table. He told them that the surface of the barely visible table represented the known, with the utensils being items of our understanding. Then, he waved his arms around, saying that everything else was the unknown.

The unknown can't be described in words. If something can be described, it's part of the known. The effects of the unknown can be witnessed but not explained. You can only point towards it. Matus asserts that it's possible to enter the unknown and witness and even use its power, but while experiences in the unknown can and do happen they can't necessarily be described or analyzed; mostly they are not even remembered.

Our identity, our personhood, is in the known part of ourselves. When the known becomes aware that it is speaking about itself, it invents words like 'I' and 'myself'. In the unknown we have no identity; we have only power and effect.

When we are born, and for a short time after, we are all unknown. We are confronted by an operating world that we must learn to share and participate in. Our known begins to develop through a total monumental effort. We can't remember this effort because it happened before we developed our identity, memory and language.

The known's importance is so encompassing that eventually we become completely invested in it, and forget what came before. We retain a vague sense of our other self, so we begin making pairs in our thinking. We think of mind and body, matter and energy, God and the Devil, but these are all singular concepts that are part of the known. They are all things that are known in some way, things that have words attached to them. They do not comprise the actual duality that our complete being is composed of, which is the known and the unknown.

The unknown can surface in our lives but only inadvertently. We can't consciously arrange to encounter it. However, the unknown can arise and when it does, the known can become aware of the totality of oneself. Usually this only happens at the moment of death.

In *Tales of Power*, Castaneda recounted how Matus taught him about the known and the unknown, and about how the known rules our lives even though it's weak in comparison to our other side, the unknown. Because of its weakness and vulnerability, the known must be cunning and ingenious in maintaining the illusion that the unknown doesn't exist. If the unknown does emerge, the known becomes vulnerable.

Anything more than a brief glimpse of the unknown is deadly for the known and, therefore, for the entire being. When the unknown emerges, it's like a 'bad dog'. Repeatedly, Matus dumped buckets of water on Castaneda to 'whip his nagual back to its place. The tonal must be protected at any cost. The crown has to be taken away from it, but it must remain as the protected overseer.'

The unknown can only emerge safely if it's used to boost

the known. When this is achieved, it's called personal power. Without long and careful training any encounter with the unknown results in the known 'crapping out', creating a fatal shock. Without training, the known prefers to die rather than give up control.

Training the known consists of removing all unnecessary items from it – 'cleaning the island of the tonal'. Any habits, thoughts, beliefs, and especially memories of relationships, that would prevent the known from surviving an encounter with the unknown, must be uncovered and released. A new internal dialog must be developed that allows for the awareness of both the known and the unknown.

Tales of Power concludes with the pivotal act on which all of Castaneda's writings hinged. In 1973, Castaneda, together with Pablito and Nestor, followed Matus and his group of sorcerers to a high plateau in the mountains of Mexico. At the edge of the plateau was a sheer cliff. This particular plateau and cliff were part of the history and folklore of Matus' sorcery tradition. Throughout history, many sorcery groups and trained warriors had come there for their ultimate and final meeting together. At the end of their training, apprentices leaped from the cliff. Castaneda did the same at the end of *Tales of Power*.

The events on the plateau marked the final appearance of don Juan and don Genaro, who also leaped but didn't come back, and the end of Castaneda's apprenticeship. Of course, we know that the author survived to tell this story and many others in future books.

Before the jump, Castaneda was given the 'sorcerers' explanation', which clarified how this act could be performed; how a person could leap off a cliff and survive.

According to this explanation, when we are in the pure

unknown we are composed of a cluster of 'feelings, beings and selves' that exist and 'float' in the unknown 'like barges, peaceful, unaltered, forever.'

Matus' explanation continued:

'Then the glue of life binds some of them together ... When the glue of life binds those feelings together a being is created, a being that loses the sense of its true nature and becomes blinded by the glare and clamor of the area where beings hover, the tonal. The tonal is where all the unified organization exists. A being pops into the tonal once the force of life has bound all the needed feelings together ... the tonal begins at birth and ends at death ... as soon as the force of life leaves the body all those single awarenesses disintegrate and go back again to where they came from, the nagual ... at death, they sink deeply and move independently as if they had never been a unit.'

THERE IS a principle in physics which states that matter cannot be created or destroyed. In the same way, Castaneda's universe is made up of units of selves and feelings, which are eternal. When the units are in the unknown, they float separately. To emerge into the known, they are collected into groups by the life force. When the being dies, the units separate again and return to float in the unknown.

When Castaneda leapt off the cliff, he did it as a trained warrior who had practiced and been prepared to venture intentionally into the unknown. Entering the unknown in this way was like dying, except that the individual units only expanded 'without losing their togetherness'. A trained warrior could then reintegrate his components in any form he knew at any location he chose.

This pivotal moment of Castaneda's learning – the leap off

the cliff – caused an unavoidable and final conflict between his reason and the totality of himself. Matus pointed out that the sorcerers' explanation 'seems harmless and charming, but ... it delivers a blow that no-one can parry'.

Leaping from the cliff was not the conclusion of Castaneda's apprenticeship. It was the end of his time with his teachers, which had lasted 13 years. But much of his learning up to this point took place in the unknown, and he couldn't remember it in his normal awareness. The remaining task of remembering and integrating all he had been taught then began, which took another decade and more.

7

FINDING THE OTHER SELF AGAIN

The fifth book, *The Second Ring of Power*, occupies a crucial position in the series, and is different from the others. It only presents one straightforward narrative of a series of events in chronological order. Castaneda returned to Mexico about 18 months after leaping off the cliff. He spent several weeks visiting the group of co-apprentices who were with him during his earlier time with Matus and Genaro. All the other Castaneda books are arranged in chapters by themes; cutting and pasting episodes from events widely separated in time and place, using conversations and partial narratives from varied isolated events.

Castaneda's leap from the cliff at the end of *Tales of Power* should have been the culmination of his apprenticeship. He had followed Matus' program to its conclusion and then performed the ultimate act. But it wasn't the end. He somehow survived the leap, and wrote the book *Tales of Power*. But in a sense he did not launch. Instead he went back to normal. His reason and common sense reasserted themselves. He found himself questioning what, if anything at all, had happened to him.

That final meeting with Matus at the cliff happened sometime in 1973. *Tales of Power* was published a year later. How Castaneda survived and returned to Los Angeles remained a mystery. Reason had to be defeated for him to survive, but a detailed description of what ensued after leaping off the cliff wouldn't appear until his final book, *The Active Side of Infinity*, 25 years later.

At the cliff in 1973 don Juan required Castaneda to say his final farewells to all the other players. It was understood that don Juan and don Genaro would leave the earth somehow at the same moment Castaneda leaped. It wasn't clear what would happen to Castaneda after the leap. His personal power would determine whether he survived; then, it was his choice to return or not.

Castaneda's common sense reasserted itself during the period he was in Los Angeles. When he returned to Mexico his reason was firmly in control again. His purpose of going back was to question Pablito and Nestor about the events at the plateau, and specifically to ask if the events actually happened or were just a dream or hallucination. He remembered that Pablito and Nestor accompanied him to the cliff and jumped along with him, but now he wasn't sure what happened there.

Upon arriving in Mexico, sometime either in 1974 or 1975, Castaneda was surprised to discover that there was a much larger group of apprentices than he was previously aware of. Not only Pablito and Nestor but also one other man and a group of five women were awaiting Castaneda's return. All of them had been apprentices to Juan Matus and Genaro Flores with Castaneda. They were anxiously awaiting Castaneda's return so they could continue and complete their mutual learning, with the aim of improving their skills together in a traditional sorcery group. They were also prepared to complete specific tasks and tests left behind for them by Matus. When Castaneda first arrived, he immediately met dona Soledad, whom he knew as Pablito's mother (as described in the first chapter).

In his earlier books, Castaneda did mention a group of women, but mistakenly believed they were bystanders or family members. They were, in fact, part of a circle of students gathered by don Juan to accompany Castaneda, Pablito and Nestor. Interactions between them and him had been very limited and controlled. They colluded with don Juan and don Genaro to conceal their participation in Castaneda's apprenticeship. The knowledge that they were part of the joint apprenticeship had been kept hidden from Castaneda.

We now learn that Matus had 'made', meaning discovered and designated, two male apprentices (Castaneda and Eligio) and five female apprentices (Lidia, Josefina, Elena, Rosa and Soledad). The women lived with Pablito and posed as his sisters. Don Genaro had made three male apprentices: Pablito, Nestor and Benigno.

This is the first of several re-interpretations of the seminal events that happened while Castaneda and Matus were together between 1960 and 1973.

We can look at this in several ways. It could have been just a Hollywood-style attempt to create sequels. The publisher and author together may have decided to find a way to pump out more books even though the story had ended; just keep going back over the same facts, but add material that supposedly was ignored the first time around.

It could also indicate a literary strategy to introduce new confidants whose information and memories illuminate facts and perspectives that weren't noticed before.

Or, thirdly, it could introduce a hypothesis about memory itself, one that makes it possible to remember and discover previously unknown things that actually happened. Events were kept in memory even though they didn't register as perceived events when they happened.

This is Castaneda's intention: to redefine how we perceive and remember experienced events. Due to the dual nature of our awareness, we select some parts of experience to be aware of and to remember consciously. All other aspects of our experience are ignored and forgotten. Those forgotten elements remain stored somewhere in our luminous being, though, and can be recovered later.

Every new book from then on introduced new characters or events from the 1960-1973 apprenticeship period. If Castaneda's theory of memory is right, it's possible that our luminous beings contain memories of events and people who were ignored and forgotten during the original experience, but stored somewhere to be remembered later. Events that are not designated as real are discarded at the time, but remain stored as deep memories that can surface again. The total accumulation of these deep memories can be greater than the sum of all that we consider to be the real memories of our lives.

Castaneda returned to Mexico to search for explanations about don Juan and don Genaro, and to confirm what had happened to him. Instead, he found himself immersed in a primitive sorcery struggle for power amongst the apprentices.

Upon his arrival in Mexico, he quickly fell into deadly combat with dona Soledad (as described in the first chapter). Before he realized what he had gotten himself into, she had her hairband twisted around his neck and was strangling him. Castaneda felt a shiver as some part of him rose above the scene. He viewed himself being murdered, seemingly from a separate position. In a rage, this separate part of him smacked dona Soledad on the forehead, causing her to release his body from her deadly grip. A ghostlike part of her flew off and huddled in the corner of the room 'like a frightened child'.

Matus had prepared and directed the other apprentices to stalk and kill Castaneda, supposedly to steal his power. Castaneda himself had asked them to do this, but forgotten. Several years earlier, while in a state of heightened awareness, Castaneda lamented that he knew he would return to normal awareness and forget that his new awareness even existed. He asked don Juan and the other apprentices to kill him rather than leave him in ignorance if that happened. They made a vow to do it, which Castaneda had forgotten about.

Matus knew that Castaneda would return to Mexico with his reason firmly in control, which meant that his gains of sorcery knowledge would be lost to him. Because Castaneda requested it, Matus instructed and prepared the other apprentices to challenge him, knowing that permanent gains in awareness only come with life-or-death challenges.

The test for Castaneda was whether his reason would prevail. If it did, he would deny the challenge and be defeated and die. If his reason relinquished control, his sorcery powers could be released to protect him, confirming and advancing his sorcery training.

Castaneda passed the tests. One after another, his power

emerged and he survived, injuring the other apprentices gravely. He then cured their wounds, which confirmed him as their leader. According to the instructions Matus left for them, they were then charged to help each other seek the requisite power and knowledge to enter 'the other world' where Matus and Genaro had gone. They needed and expected Castaneda to lead them.

WHEN JUAN MATUS first encountered Castaneda and designated him as his successor to hand over his knowledge to, he also assembled this group of five women and three men to join and support him. The evolution of a sorcerer is too arduous and dangerous to be accomplished alone. Just as Castaneda had his original story about first meeting Juan Matus, all the other sorcery apprentices had compelling stories about their first encounters with the sorcerers' world, and transitions from their previous lives.

The five women were known as the 'little sisters'. Matus found Lidia and Josefina while visiting small villages in the mountains. Lidia was abandoned in a barn, extremely ill. Genaro took her into his house and cared for her. Matus found Josefina while visiting a healer. She was known as a crazy girl who did nothing but cry all the time, and her family was happy to leave her with don Juan when he offered to cure her. Rosa bumped into Matus while chasing a pig on a country road, and started yelling at him. Sorcerers are not meant to bump into people unawares, so Matus viewed their encounter as an omen. He shouted back at her, and challenged her to drop everything and join him when he left the area at noon that day, and she did.

Elena had two daughters with an abusive husband, and became obese. Another man lured her away to a different city, got her pregnant again, and forced her to beg on the street with a sick baby in her arms. When she ran away and went back looking for her two daughters, her first husband's family stoned her and left her for dead. She met Pablito while hitchhiking, and he took her in to work in his laundry business, where Matus found her. They renamed her La Gorda – the fat girl.

Dona Soledad was not strictly a member of the group. She was originally known as Manuelita, and posed as Pablito's mother. Since sorcery was taboo in Mexico then, and therefore dangerous, the apprentices had to carry on elaborate ruses to hide what they were doing. That's why they lived together in one house, posing as a family. They carried out their impersonations with great fervor, as this was also a sorcerers' discipline, called 'stalking', which will be described later.

According to Matus, women make better sorcerers than men. Women find it much easier to disappear from their former lives, because in traditional societies their families don't depend on them to carry on the family name or business. They can often easily disappear, unlike men whose families will usually not let them go away easily.

According to Pablito, all the women in Castaneda's group were in desperate straits when they met Matus. The male apprentices, he claimed, who were known as 'the Genaros', were living normal lives, 'well and alive and happy'.

Working in a market, Pablito fell in love with a girl who worked near him. He built her family a merchant's booth with a hidden space where the two lovers could hide and make love.

Genaro and Matus saw the table shaking every day and flushed him out. When Pablito realized how strong don Juan was, he hired him as a laborer, and Matus played along. Then, Genaro told him Matus was strong because of a secret potion he could make, and convinced Pablito to start a business together.

Benigno was one of five young men Castaneda and Matus met in the desert on one of their walks. Eligio lived nearby and knew Matus from childhood. When he heard about the American apprentice (Castaneda) he came to Matus' house to meet him on the day Matus was planning to give peyote to his grandson. Instead of hooking his grandson, Matus got Eligio. Eligio made an instant connection with the sorcerers' world, and therefore was not considered an apprentice in training. Nestor was a healer who bought herbs from don Genaro. When he stalked Genaro into the hills, trying to discover his supplier's source, he was struck by lightning, and had to be cured by Genaro.

THE EIGHT APPRENTICES, accepted now as Castaneda's cohorts, set up a series of meetings to exhibit their respective powers to each other. They hoped to create a sorcerers' traditional grouping.

The women performed a series of actions in which they became pure balls of energy. They grabbed onto lines of energy and used them to leap or fly, or to hide behind. Castaneda watched, but just like with Genaro Flores on the waterfall, he could only perceive their human images performing impossible acrobatic feats. His reason continued to assert itself and prevent him from seeing.

It was frustrating for the group of young apprentices. Castaneda was meant to be their peerless leader, but he kept behaving like a beginner or, worse, an outsider. After a long struggle, they reluctantly accepted his limitations. Even though his powers could emerge when there was a life-or-death struggle, he couldn't sustain his ability to see, so it was obvious he couldn't lead their group. This meant they couldn't progress further on their quests, and their prior training was useless.

Finally, in a dramatic showdown, they forgave Castaneda and put aside their expectations. At that moment, Castaneda's ears popped. He re-remembered the events he had earlier witnessed. In this new remembering, he saw the pure balls and lines of energy that the women had used to perform their magic. He could see, as opposed to look at, them for the first time.

Castaneda's struggle revealed the central paradox of perception. In the two-step process which comprises perception, where we are constantly recollecting, we have two separate sets of perceived data, but we choose to see and remember only one.

As Castaneda said, he was 'too lazy to remember what I had seen; therefore I only bothered with what I had looked at ... It is hard to believe that I can remember now something I didn't remember at all a while ago.'

He concluded that all of us look and see at the same time, but 'we choose not to remember what we see'. In the two-step process of perception, we always see first, but immediately ignore what we see to focus only on what we look at instead. This act of perception is 'the core of our being'.

As we grow up, we develop our attention. Attention is the ability to 'hold the images of the world'. Once we can perceive the agreed world and hold it in place, our perception becomes a constantly repeating two-step process which always produces the same being in the same world.

The first step is the raw act of perception, in which the cocoon of aware energy interacts with other aware energy. The second step is our magical ability to set aside the primary perception and then impose the familiar images of our normal world onto what we are seeing. We always perceive the agreed-on images of our real world, the world we agree is real. We do this with others who've been taught the same. We all forcefully deny that any such thing would even be possible.

When an assemblage point fixes itself in a position inside the cocoon and aligns the energy that goes through it, the result is a dream. We are all dreamers dreaming together. This is the basic act for all sentient beings, this act of magic. Every species and sort of being does the same. We are born perceivers, inserted into being at one particular place, but capable of perceiving many worlds. We learn to perceive one world exclusively, intensively, and as completely as possible. To hold the images of the one agreed-on world, we think about it and talk about it over and over, broadening and deepening our understanding of our projected world, and call that intelligence.

The exclusive awareness of the ordinary world is first achieved in childhood, not long after birth. We keep our focus steady throughout life by a constant effort. We are normally unaware of this effort that keeps our world assembled, just as we are unaware of the autonomic nervous system that keeps our body breathing and functioning.

We engage and entangle ourselves with the agreed-on world through language, images and symbols. With these we produce a constant stream of interior and exterior dialog, through which we maintain and continually refresh our aware-

ness of our world. This conscious and subconscious mainte-
nance of our attention monopolizes our energy, leaving nothing
left.

Another way to describe this process is to say there are two
types of attention. The 'first attention' is our awareness of the
agreed-on real world. At birth, we didn't have this attention. It
had to be developed. We learnt very early in life how to hold
onto the images of the agreed-on real world, and once engaged
with it we were taught to never question it. We hooked
ourselves into the 'ring of power' that engaged us fully with that
world. All our energy and complete sense of self were assigned
to that ring of power.

The first attention is paying attention to the known. The
'second attention' is the attention of the unknown, which we
keep out of awareness. Just before the moment of death, the
loss of life energy causes the two-step process of perception to
stop. The second attention emerges then, along with all the
hidden memories contained in it, and an inexplicable universe
is revealed.

There is a way to reach the second attention during life by
utilizing the three intermediary processes of the eight point
diagram: dreaming, seeing, and feeling.

Just as there were no standard steps for reaching the first
attention in childhood, there are also none for the second attention. It must be done with a total effort, born of a clear and
persistent intention to get there. It needs to be a matter of life
and death, which is why Matus set it up for the apprentices to
kill Castaneda. Without the impetus of a life-or-death situation,
humans won't reach the second attention.

8

DREAMING TOGETHER

Because this is a series of books, Castaneda re-introduced himself at the beginning of each successive one, to review prior material, to remind the continuing reader where he left off, and to bring new readers up to speed. He used these re-introductions also to explain how his understanding of Matus' teachings changed over time.

In the prologue to his sixth book, *The Eagle's Gift*, first published in 1981, Castaneda redefined some of Matus' terms. He explained that he started his relationship with Matus as an anthropologist studying the uses of psychedelic plants. After that his understanding changed, and he considered that he was being taught sorcery. Then eventually he learned that Matus and Genaro were not really sorcerers; they were 'practitioners of an ancient knowledge' that was related to sorcery, but no longer the same as sorcery had been in the past. Castaneda changed from being an intellectual who studied anthropological phenomena into a participant. At this point, as reflected in his books, his work had 'transformed into an autobiography'. He assured the reader that his adventures were 'not fiction'; they seem unreal because they are foreign to us.

THE PREVIOUS BOOK, *The Second Ring of Power*, showed Castaneda being forced to move from the first attention to the second attention by life-or-death struggles. *The Eagle's Gift* is about the next step: moving from the first to the second attention without the impetus of a deadly encounter. This book describes techniques to intentionally move from the first attention into the second once a commitment is made to do so.

The division of human awareness into the first and second attentions isn't an aberration or corruption. It reflects the division of awareness in the universe. A basic pairing of opposites exists everywhere, as the tonal and the nagual, the known and the unknown.

The human known is made up of everything we consider to be part of our life, everything we remember, and everything our intellect can conceive. It's defined by our senses and language, and ruled mainly by reason. The known's awareness is called the 'first attention'; another name is the 'right-side awareness'.

Even though the awareness of the unknown is primary in the sense that it was with us at birth, it's called the second attention because it was learned about after we became proficient in the first attention. The second attention is also known as 'left-side awareness'. Left-side awareness is awareness of the unknown when we encounter the vast ocean of awareness. It is 'a realm of indescribable features: a realm impossible to contain in words'. In the unknown, we perceive with our entire being. The unknown is not constricted by reason. It's beyond language and can't be described with words.

Reason and language only comprise a small part of the totality of our selves. In the other, much vaster, part another kind of knowledge exists without reason and language.

Left-side awareness knows about the right side, but the right side, where we normally spend our lives, is usually not aware of the left side. If we are ever in the left side, whatever happens to us there is forgotten when we return to the right side. Like a drunk on the morning after, or a patient in hypnotherapy or under anesthesia, there can be events that happened and periods of time where a curtain is drawn. Images and data are missing from memory which can take a huge effort to remember. It's usually impossible to remember but Castaneda says that if someone else was there with us they can later help to trigger our memory, or they can help us through deduction to get close enough so that related details are there to cause the recollections to emerge.

In one sense, memory is really the main topic of the entire Castaneda opus. Memory, not hallucinogens, is the key to other states of consciousness. But memory isn't what we think it is. Our normal memory is more like a denial of memory; it's only a small selective recollection of a few items that our rationality and identity have chosen as their flag to rally around. A vast reservoir exists beyond that where memories of the other self are, in the second attention. The luminous body stores memories starting from the moment of birth; they are part of the other self, unacceptable to the first attention and the normal self.

The second attention, also known as the other self, the left side or the unknown, is aware of the first attention, which is the normal self, the right side or the known. But the first attention, the right side, is not aware of the left side. The task for us is to make the first attention accept the existence of the second attention, to remember the totality of one's self.

Consciousness is unevenly divided into three parts. The smallest is the first attention, the known world and the physical body, and the everyday attention needed to deal with normal life.

The second attention is a much larger domain. It remains in the background for most of our lives, only surfacing through trauma, medical or chemical intervention, or deliberate training. The second attention reveals itself at death for all of us, when the first attention no longer has the energy to assert itself. The second attention encompasses all our denied perceptions and stored memories, and the awareness and remembrance of ourselves and others as luminous cocoons.

Our life in the first attention is composed of challenges that are meant to lead us to the second attention. The second attention is the battleground for reaching the largest and final third attention. The third attention is not described in Castaneda's work; according to Matus, it is where he and Genaro intended to go at the same moment Castaneda jumped off the cliff.

THE NARRATIVE FROM the previous book continued into *The Eagle's Gift*. Castaneda and the eight other apprentices continued to confront each other in a struggle for power. The others expected Castaneda to act as their leader, but gradually discovered, as he repeatedly disappointed them, that he was on a different trajectory. Every time they confronted each other with their respective powers, Castaneda rallied himself to protect his own life by injuring them. Gradually, their interactions guided them to a house in another town in central Mexico where they all encountered powerful but seemingly impossible memories.

They somehow recalled spending a lot of time in that house. Then they remembered that there was another teacher who led them, in addition to Matus and Genaro, and that was his house. His name was Silvio Manuel. Manuel had also taught them, in that house, but they had no memories of him. They deduced that every time they encountered Manuel, they had been in the second attention and, therefore, all awareness of him was forgotten.

Gradually, they figured out, through a combination of reasoning and remembering, that Matus and Genaro intentionally allowed themselves to be with Castaneda and the young apprentices in their normal first attention many times. But at the same time there had also been an older group of sorcerers surrounding Matus, who the younger group had no memories of meeting. They met them occasionally but only in the second attention; they had no memories of this group in their first attention.

As a teaching strategy, the older sorcerers made the apprentices witness events and accept explanations from the larger group of teachers in the second attention only. The apprentices never met those teachers in the first attention, or even heard mention of the old teachers' names while in the first attention. Their very existence was unknown in the normal daily awareness of the young apprentices.

If the events and teachings from the larger group of teachers had been encountered in the first attention, reason would have intervened and challenged or rejected anything it did not consider to be real and verifiable. The teachings would not have sunk in. By teaching the apprentices in the second attention, the old sorcerers directly imparted their knowledge to the students in a state of mind where everything would be immediately understood and accepted. In that state of mind, the teachings were experienced directly and then stored in memory without the interference of reason. Even though the teachings would be forgotten, they would be stored faithfully in the luminous body.

The apprentices were then left on their own, back in the first attention, with the seemingly impossible task of remembering what they learned, like a subject of hypnosis trying to remember what happened while under hypnosis. The challenge given to students by this teaching method is the challenge we all face in recovering the totality of ourselves.

The apprentices remembered that Castaneda had a special relationship with Silvio Manuel; in fact, he had been seriously injured and Manuel saved his life. They suspected that Manuel had enslaved Castaneda somehow, and Castaneda was now trying to enslave them in turn. These and other confusing memories revealed to all that they didn't belong together. They parted ways, abruptly and finally, except for one woman, La Gorda, who continued to spend time with Castaneda. He left the group and returned to Los Angeles. Later, he joined up with La Gorda alone in Arizona.

THIS REALIGNMENT, the separation from the young apprentices, started a new cycle of learning, where Castaneda and La Gorda worked together in Arizona and Los Angeles as equals. They explored a new world that they managed to open by deduction, and then investigate in their dreams.

The only way for the first attention to remember items from the second attention is through dreaming. Because they had shared experiences in the second attention, they assumed they should be able to dream together and, by doing so, remember things together.

To dream together they needed to be asleep at the same time, though not necessarily in the same location. They knew that their teachers had discussed dreaming together; it happened spontaneously if there was a shared intent. Because each of them separately had already learned the basics of dreaming – which would be spelled out in Castaneda's later book, *The Art of Dreaming* – they gradually figured out how to meet up in shared dreams and then explore those dreams together, uncovering memories they shared while in the other self.

According to Castaneda, by dreaming together he and La Gorda were recapitulating what all humans do as infants when we learn to join the world our elders impart to us. The luminous cocoon naturally and spontaneously dreams together with other cocoons, meaning they spontaneously put their assemblage points at the same positions. The participants can then agree on the contents of the world they share, which makes it real to them. Dreaming together is what we do when we join any world; it is also the procedure don Juan's seers used to remember information and memories that were stored in the second attention.

One goal of don Juan's sorcery training method was to create shared memories in the second attention among the apprentices. Castaneda and La Gorda knew they had the same shared but hidden memories, because they knew don Juan set it up like that. Once they found themselves in a shared dream, by exploring it together it became real to them; to be real means to be agreed on with someone. Once that shared dream was real it became part of the first attention and was remembered. It could then release other related memories in a flood.

In their dreams together Castaneda and La Gorda met in a shared but forgotten memory, where they found themselves in a big house in Mexico with a large group of sorcerers, including Matus and Genaro. Memories are stored in very precise positions of the assemblage point. By meeting in a dream, they spontaneously located the same precise position of the assemblage point together. Then, they shared continuing awareness in that memory as it unfolded in a re-enactment. They relived memories which were previously lost to them. According to Castaneda, memories that are relocated in this way can be relived with even more clarity and intensity than the original experience had.

Castaneda and La Gorda remembered that Matus and Genaro were not alone but part of a large group of sorcerers, and that Castaneda and La Gorda, and the other apprentices, had been with that group many times. But who were these people? What happened? How could they have forgotten?

At this point in the ongoing narrative Castaneda, aided by La Gorda, claimed an entire previously unknown history of his own life by remembering things in dreams and bringing these previously unknown memories into his normal awareness.

A cynic must ask: what is this continual retroactive introduction of new events and characters into the past? Is this another publishing gimmick to ensure his series of profitable books continues? Or is the relationship between the first and second attentions, and the recovery of lost memories and worlds from the second attention, the hinge that opens the entire scope of Castaneda's complete works? Does this lead to the center of Castaneda's philosophy?

If the underlying philosophy of the cocoons and filaments of energy is true, then all of Castaneda's stories are possible and much more beyond. If the universe is composed of aware energy and holds a multitude of assemblage points where perception can be assembled into many worlds, then our partial mastery of our one point of perception, though absolutely crucial to our survival, is a small matter indeed. If our known world is just a tiny island in a vast unknown and inconceivable universe, then the only worthy activity for us is to organize our island as our launch pad from which we explore the vast unknown.

Castaneda and La Gorda proceeded through a combined process of deduction, dreaming together, and remembering to conclude that many things happened to them with Matus and his contemporaries which they had forgotten.

They deduced that they had experienced most of their apprenticeship in the second attention. They remembered they had been apprentices under a large family of teachers, including Matus, Genaro, Manuel and 13 others. These additional sorcerers conducted their teachings exclusively while the students were in the second attention. Students somehow were forced into the second attention when interacting with the large group of old sorcerers.

In the first attention, students were only allowed to be with Matus and Genaro, so they duly remembered interactions with those two. For Castaneda and La Gorda to remember all the other teachers and their experiences with them, they had to access both their first and second attentions together.

In fact, this was the teaching method itself. Acquiring the ability to move between the first and second attentions was the goal. Their old teachers gave them information directly, but it was information that would've been unacceptable to reason and, therefore, rejected by the first attention. So, the information was given to them while in the second attention and stored there.

The teachers in don Juan Matus' group were able to control the attention of the students. They could somehow move the assemblage points of many students to the exact same spot at the same time. In doing this, they set up the students for a lifetime of re-learning the information they had stored, thereby putting that information in the first attention. By remembering, they would achieve understanding and control of both sides of their awareness, arriving at the totality of themselves. Through this effort, they learnt how to move their own assemblage points, thereby completing their training.

AT THIS POINT in the narrative, around the middle of *The Eagle's Gift*, Castaneda's tone of voice changed abruptly. Prior to this, the story of Carlos Castaneda and don Juan had been about an uncertain and fumbling apprentice who kept moving forward despite himself – full of doubts and questions. Once Castaneda remembered his other self with La Gorda's assistance, his tone of voice changed.

He could now see the entire scope of the task of learning and remembering that don Juan Matus left for him. He remembered and understood the historical information don Juan gave him about their shared heritage. He began to confidently recount the myth of the ancient sorcerers' way of life and the history of sorcery.

By recovering a series of memories from their time with Matus, Castaneda and La Gorda discovered that they had been joined with their eight contemporary apprentices in an effort to form a traditional grouping of sorcerers according to an ancient tradition, referred to as the Toltec Tradition. Also called the tradition of 'the ancient sorcerers of Mexico', this had evolved into something called the tradition of the 'new seers' or the 'men of knowledge'. Don Juan Matus, Genaro Flores and their contemporary cohorts were new seers. They no longer considered themselves sorcerers, but they came from the sorcery tradition.

According to this tradition, there was a vast period of human civilization on the American continents, especially in Mexico, that was led by a group that Matus calls the ancient sorcerers of Mexico or the Toltecs. The religion of this culture, according to the tradition, started as far back as 10,000 years ago and centred on the exploration and manipulation of the second attention.

This original Toltec civilization reached its height in the period between 5000 and 2000 BCE, located around the Valley of Mexico. It was then conquered by a different civilization that wasn't named, but was possibly the Maya. The Toltec religion continued to exist under the new regime, but over time became corrupt, weak and vulnerable

Sorcerers had always been notorious for using their knowledge to control and take advantage of their fellow men. The more the religion decayed, the more it became only known for its excesses and bad behavior. It barely survived until the Spanish Conquest. With their superior technology, Christianity and Inquisition, the Spanish hunted down and exterminated all remaining Toltec sorcerers they could find.

Isolated groups survived the Inquisition, with strict new rules assuring absolute secrecy. Kept alive in small and separate groups and withstanding the difficult conditions of oppression, a new, stronger and better organized version of the old beliefs emerged. It avoided and eschewed using sorcery to control or manipulate other people, which only brought violence and destruction in response. This new version is the 'new seers' or the 'men of knowledge'. Don Juan Matus' group were 'new seers'; their secret lineage went back 27 generations.

IN THE NEW version of the ancient Toltec religion, groups of apprentice warriors lived in isolation from other groups. From generation to generation, each troupe was gathered, sponsored and trained by an older generation, who mirrored them in number and character. The trained sorcerers in the older group could move freely from one attention to the other. They could also manipulate the awareness of students by moving the students' awareness from the first to the second attention and back again.

Once they gathered their group of apprentices, the sorcerers manipulated the students into the second attention, and then directly and quickly transmitted their teachings, which were stored in the students' second attention.

The students reverted to the first attention, where all the teaching was forgotten. The older generation then left the world, either by dying or going into the third attention. The younger students were scattered and had to find each other again while in the first attention. They had to help each other remember what they learned in the second attention from their teachers, like Castaneda and La Gorda did. In this way, the first attention allowed the second to come into its awareness through remembering and dreaming.

Once the second attention, the other self, is uncovered and integrated into the first attention, the man or woman who has accomplished that gains access to the totality of themselves, and can 'go directly to the memories of our luminosity with unfathomable results'.

The memories of our luminosity can include family, tribal and racial memories that have been passed on for generations. Because memories can be stored in positions of the assemblage point, they can be unconsciously transmitted for generations through the processes of dreaming together with parents and elders. The assemblage point not only selects and assembles perception, it also stores perception. Memories are kept in precise positions of the assemblage point, and can be unknowingly passed on for generations.

THROUGH THEIR INTERACTION with the warriors of the older generation in the second attention, apprentices are given a 'ledge to stand on' in the unknown. A small outpost of the other self is cultivated and left in place 'by deliberately filling it with memories of interaction. The memories are forgotten only to resurface someday in order to serve as a rational outpost from where to depart into the immeasurable vastness of the other self.'

By the end of *The Eagle's Gift*, Castaneda rediscovered the 'ledge to stand on' that his teachers helped him construct. He also remembered all the events that led to his separation from the young group of warriors he studied with. Those apprentices were now left without a leader, and Castaneda went along his own path separate from them.

9

COCOONS AND FILAMENTS

Castaneda's seventh and eighth books, *The Fire from Within* and *The Power of Silence*, were published in 1984 and 1987. In these two books, Castaneda finally provided a clear summary of the philosophy behind his writing.

This was about 25 years after his first meeting with Matus (in 1960), more than 16 years after his first book was published (1968), and more than a decade after his apprenticeship with Matus ended in 1973.

It took him all that time and effort to reach this point. In uncovering this philosophy, he finally revealed a deep consistency which redefined and clarified all his previous writing. Questions about the veracity and origins of his stories remained, but the gaps of inconsistency and incoherence were closed. Before this, critics could say, whether fact or fiction, that it didn't make sense. After this, they had to say that it did make sense, though the question remained whether it was fact, fiction, or stolen.

For the purposes of this book, I already introduced an explanation in the fourth chapter, *Emanations of Intent*. For earlier readers, like me, reading the books one by one as they were published, the explanation did not arrive until this point. Before this point was reached, it's understandable that Castaneda would be considered by many to be simply another exhibitionist writer from the 1960s and 1970s purveying new-age hallucinogenic pseudo-philosophy simply to sell books.

The Fire from Within and *The Power of Silence* together comprise the summation of don Juan's teachings to the extent of Castaneda's understanding, which was not complete. Castaneda acknowledged his achievement was insufficient, and in his further works until the end it continued to be so.

MAN HAS two types of awareness, said Castaneda again: the right and left sides. This reflects the way the universe is divided into the known and the unknown. Matus' teachings were, therefore, also divided into two parts: teachings for the right side and teachings for the left side. Teachings for the right side were acceptable to our reason, while teachings for the left side were not.

Teachings for the right side were conducted while Castaneda was in his normal state of awareness. Those teachings were written about in the first six books.

Matus had the ability to intentionally force Castaneda's awareness to switch from one side to the other. Whenever don Juan wanted to demonstrate or teach something that would not be accepted by Castaneda's normal rational self, Matus made him change to the left side. After the lesson was over, Matus moved Castaneda back to the right side, where he promptly forgot what he had just seen and heard. The teaching, though, remained stored somewhere in the left side, to be recovered later. Matus carefully organized his teachings so that Castaneda would remain with the task of remembering them after the teacher was gone. In this remembering, Castaneda would uncover his other self, thereby completing his training.

After his apprenticeship ended and Matus was gone, Castaneda and La Gorda together figured out how to access the hidden memories Matus had placed in storage for them. They started to remember the teachings for the left side.

Castaneda knew then, finally, that during his years as an apprentice there was a group of 16 people who taught him on the left side. They didn't call themselves sorcerers, or call their teachings sorcery; rather, they taught 'how to master three aspects of an ancient knowledge they possessed: awareness, stalking, and intent. And they were not sorcerers, they were seers.'

They came from a tradition that grew out of what they called 'ancient sorcery', but over time that tradition evolved beyond sorcery into something more modern.

Matus described human history from the left side, telling of an 'ancient chain of knowledge that extended over thousands of years ... ages before the Spaniards came to Mexico.' The men and women of this tradition knew how to 'fixate the awareness' of other people, using 'secret knowledge' to dominate their societies.

These powerful sorcerers ruled the peoples of ancient Mexico until the area was conquered, first by other native

American groups, then by the Spanish. The Spaniards systematically exterminated the remaining sorcerers. Only small
dispersed groups survived. They set up separate lineages to
secretly preserve the ancient knowledge and traditions, but
considered the overall ancient belief system to have failed. They
renamed themselves the 'new seers'.

In yet another progressive re-defining of terms, Castaneda
now defined sorcery as the ability to force other people to
change their awareness using secret knowledge. The old
sorcerers used these powers to dominate and control their societies. The new seers still had these abilities, but only used them
to help others gain freedom.

Writing more than a decade after Matus' departure,
Castaneda had progressed in his remembering to the point
where he was able to recall and retrieve the basic teaching that
he received from Matus, which he called the 'mastery of awareness.' By remembering his experiences in the second attention,
he gained access to the totality of himself.

Being able to move freely from the first to the second attention and back again is the mastery of awareness, which makes
the totality of one's self available and accessible.

Up to this point, Castaneda continually asserted that his
work and experiences were true, as he perceived them over
time. But because his understanding and perception was
incomplete his rendering of events seemed haphazardly organized, with disjointed chronologies and no discernible underlying philosophy. Whether considered as fact or fiction, his
storytelling could be rightfully criticized as being full of
inconsistencies and contradictions regarding times and
places. But once he achieved the totality of himself everything could be tied up in one view for the first time. Looking

back at his work from this viewpoint, there are no inconsistencies.

The knowledge taught to him by the new seers included the mastery of awareness, the art of stalking, and the mastery of intent.

The mastery of awareness was about the two selves and the two types of awareness, and how after an untold struggle they were integrated through memory, so the totality of one's self was realized. The art of stalking was about managing behavior to intentionally and harmoniously break up the flow of habitual events and perceptions in normal awareness. The mastery of intent was about discovering and nurturing our connection to the 'spirit', the flow of universal aware energy, until it could be summoned and utilized at will.

Castaneda said he was given the full teaching for all three topics in the second attention. He had managed to remember the first, the mastery of awareness, but never recovered and elucidated the other two sets of teachings in his written work: the art of stalking and the mastery of intent.

His failure to master the art of stalking might partially explain the often clumsy presentation of his story as autobiography. Castaneda most likely meant to increase the impact and intensity of his depiction of the ancient sorcerers, by inserting himself and other contemporaries into the story. He intended to reveal a truth that would not have come through in a dry dissertation.

In the end, his effort to bring the ancient tradition of sorcery and magic to life only partially succeeded. He failed to achieve what he said were the maximal qualities of a successful stalking maneuver: ruthlessness, cunning, patience and sweetness. He was not ruthless enough with his own habits and personal characteristics to clear his own history. If he had kept his personal story out of the way, or kept his personal history more impeccable, he might have succeeded better at making the myth of don Juan Matus. It shouldn't matter whether don Juan really existed, like it doesn't matter if Achilles really existed, but it is a constant topic of debate.

Don Juan repeatedly explained to Castaneda that there were two basic types of sorcerers. One sought adventure, including power over other beings, while the other sought freedom, and eschewed influencing others. According to Matus, virtually all the sorcerers of antiquity were the adventurous types, and most of them never even conceived of the new seers' quest for freedom. Matus and his group were all new seers concerned with individual freedom. Matus' own teacher, Julian Osorio, was an adventurer sorcerer who never learned to see, and may have died the death of a normal man. Matus thought Castaneda had much in common with Osorio and the ancient sorcerers.

THE FULL AND final version of the mastery of awareness was gradually developed in *The Fire from Within*. Then, in the introduction to *The Power of Silence* Castaneda formally summarised '... *the mastery of awareness, which was the cornerstone of his teachings, and which consist of the following basic premises:*

1.The universe is an infinite agglomeration of energy fields, resembling threads of light.

2.These energy fields, called the eagle's emanations, radiate from a source of inconceivable proportions, metaphorically called the Eagle.

3.Human beings are also composed of an incalculable number of the same threadlike energy fields. These eagle's emanations form an encased agglomeration that manifests itself as a ball of light the size of the person's body with the arms extended laterally, like a giant luminous egg.

4.Only a very small group of the energy fields inside this luminous ball are lit up by a point of intense brilliance located on the ball's surface.

5.Perception occurs when the energy fields in that small group immediately surrounding the point of brilliance extend their light to illuminate identical energy fields outside the ball. Since the only energy fields perceivable are those lit by the point of brilliance, that point is named "the point where perception is assembled" or simply "the assemblage point".

6.The assemblage point can be moved from its usual position on the surface of the luminous ball to another position on the surface, or into the interior. Since the brilliance of the assemblage point can light up whatever energy field it comes in contact with, when it moves to a new position it immediately brightens up new energy fields, making them perceivable. This perception is known as seeing.

7.When the assemblage point shifts, it makes possible the perception of an entirely different world – as objective and factual as the one we normally perceive. Sorcerers go into that other world to get energy, power, solutions to general and particular problems, or to face the unimaginable.

8.Intent is the pervasive force that causes us to perceive. We do not become aware because we perceive; rather, we perceive as a result of the pressure and intrusion of intent.

9.The aim of sorcerers is to reach a state of total awareness in order to experience all the possibilities of perception available to man. This state of awareness even implies an alternative way of dying.'

THE FORCE or energy in the aware filaments, which are the basic elements of the universe, is incomprehensible to us. The closest we can come to understanding that energy is to see it as the universe's intent. Somehow, it expresses the intent of the universe. Those filaments can also be called the universe's commands. They command us to be, and command us to perceive; in fact, they command everything everywhere.

The universe's intent forces us to perceive. Our entire existence and being is determined by the commands of its strings of energy, which express its intent. The universe's intent creates the cocoon and fills it with energy, and then puts the assemblage point in its place on the surface of that cocoon, commanding the being to perceive at that position.

The perceiver learns to hold the assemblage point firmly and steadily at that point and prevent it from moving. The resulting alignment produces a being living in a world. That being develops his or her own intent and identity, which pursues its own objectives and forgets where it came from, and for what purpose, and even that it is connected to the universe's intent.

During dreaming, the assemblage point dislodges itself from its fixed position and moves around. The person dreaming cannot control where the assemblage point initially moves. He or she can intend to align the energy encountered at any new position and hold it steady in that new place. If this new place is far enough from the previous place, the magic of perception will align a new world and a new perceiver simultaneously. A being will pop into existence in another world.

From our perspective, it's impossible to say where that other world is. It might be infinity, or on the other side of the universe, or right next to us but in another dimension. It really can only correctly be said to be at that position of the assemblage point. The universe has untold billions of positions where assemblage points can assemble strands of aware energy. At any position where a particular selection of countless energy strands is assembled is where that world is, and that being, and that event. To return to that world and that event, it is necessary to return to that precise position of the assemblage point.

From the dreamer's point of view, he has travelled to another world, somewhere out there in infinity, through his connection with the universe, which is his assemblage point, by aligning new strings of energy which stretch out to infinity. The dreamer's departure point was also a place somewhere in infinity, and must be returned to by finding the exact position of the assemblage point where our normal world exists.

The experiences encountered at the new position of the assemblage point are stored there. Memories and information are stored at very precise positions of the assemblage point. Once put in storage, the dreamer can later return to that point and relive that experience exactly as it happened before and have access to the knowledge there, with greater clarity and intensity than was originally.

WHEN A DREAMER BEGINS to explore new worlds, by reaching new positions of the assemblage point, he gets on a path, which is familiar to other experienced dreamers. There are milestones on the early parts of the path that all dreamers necessarily pass through. There are several proximal positions that he will encounter early in his ventures. One of these initial destinations is the position of the mold of man.

The mold of man is an entity, neither male nor female, which shapes the force of life into human form. Every form of life has a mold, which exists at a position of the assemblage point near to the one normally used. The mold of man can be encountered when the assemblage point shifts, either in dreaming or due to illness, shock or another occasion when we have sufficient power. All of us see it at the moment of death, when our life energy is gone and we can no longer hold our assemblage point still and control our perception. It appears as a 'radiant, luminous being'.

According to Matus, the mold of man is a cluster of emanations in the band of every man and woman. It is 'the portion of the eagle's emanations that seers can see directly without any danger to themselves.'

The mold was seen by the ancient sorcerers, and has been seen by many mystics throughout human history. According to Matus, the ancient sorcerers mistook it as a protector or friendly spirit that could grant favors, protection, or powers. Mystics saw the mold of man and misinterpreted it as being our god.

If we are in its presence, our self-centeredness makes us project our most cherished characteristics onto it: love, forgiveness, charisma, understanding, justice, truth. In comparison to this projection, we feel ourselves as unworthy, villainous, sinful, and evil.

The mystical experience, wherein one encounters the mold of man, is a chance seeing caused by a random movement of the assemblage point. It's a one-shot affair, after which the mystic remembers the vision and feelings of awe and reverence, and assumes that he was in the presence of humanity's god. One short vision of this sort can result in a lifetime of nostalgia.

The new seers made a point of seeing the mold many times. By seeing it repeatedly they determined that it is not a god. The mold has no power to do anything other than stamp us out as humans. It can't reward or punish us, or intervene on our behalf in any way. It is simply a pattern of energy that stamps human qualities onto aware energy, like a die that reproduces human beings. But we are not created from nothing by it, and it can't favor or help us in any way.

To free their assemblage points for further exploration, the new seers intentionally viewed the mold many times to see it for what it really is. As part of that process of liberation, the force the mold normally leaves in the body, called the human form, is scared off and detaches itself. After the human form is gone, the seer can look at himself and his perceptions with more emotional detachment, which enhances his freedom.

WHEN THE INTENT of the energy inside the cocoon aligns itself with the energy from outside, it is briefly aligned with universal intent. Through repetition, the intent inside the cocoon becomes familiar with the universe's intent, so the universe's intent can become our intent. When a person's intent merges with universal intent or command his or her assemblage point can then go to somewhere they intend. Matus says, 'our command becomes the eagle's command.'

During his or her life, a sorcerer – defined as one who can move his assemblage point with his intent – can gradually move it around within his cocoon to eventually contact and light up all the energy inside the cocoon that is in man's band. Once this is accomplished, the entire cocoon is lit up from within in a flash and becomes like a huge conductor of channelled energy. The being enters the third attention, which is an alternative way of dying. This is called 'burning with the fire from within'.

In our current monotheistic religions, there is one way of dying, with two paths after death. A person dies and then is judged by God, and either goes to heaven or hell for eternity. In Castaneda's theology, there is no god to teach and judge us; there is no heaven or hell, or evil.

According to Castaneda, it's possible to die in two ways, and it's also possible to extend existence in several ways.

One can die in the first attention, where the elements that have been gathered by the force of life simply separate and float off into the unknown, as if they had never been together.

Alternatively, after a lifetime exploring the second attention, one can go into the third attention by burning from within. Don Juan said he was sure that thousands of seers accomplished this and entered on a 'definitive journey', keeping their life force, with infinity as their new realm. He believed that their awareness would last as long as the earth existed, and they would die when the earth died.

An even larger number of sorcerers, though, including almost all the ancient sorcerers of Mexico, also did not die, according to Matus. Instead, while trying to navigate through the second attention they stumbled into realms that are arguably worse than death. Due to misguided efforts to prolong their lives, most of them ended up lost, kidnapped or imprisoned, somewhere in infinity.

∾

To venture in the unknown is a challenge for humans, and Castaneda said the purpose of life is to enrich awareness by including parts of the unknown into the area of the known. This brings us close to the universe's intention to know itself. New types of perception also bring new energy.

Matus said that his system provided the best answer to 'the question that has always haunted man: the reason for our existence'. Our rationality cannot come up with an answer to this without involving a blind leap of faith. According to Matus, the universe actively bestows awareness upon sentient beings so that the sentient beings can enhance the awareness during the process of life, and then return the awareness to the universe in an enhanced condition. The reason for existence is to enhance awareness, on behalf of the universe.

Matus said this is a fact that can be witnessed, not just a belief. The traditional Mexican sorceric way to interpret this is to glimpse 'the eagle', a projected image of the bestower of awareness that gives awareness to beings at birth and then 'eats' the enhanced awareness when the being dies.

A universal force loans a primal awareness to sentient beings. It continually attracts that awareness back towards itself while the awareness is being enriched and enhanced during life. The living being resists this attraction during life until it is exhausted and the universal force disintegrates the living being and recovers the awareness again, enhanced by that lifetime's experiences. At the moment of death, all of life's experiences are released from where they were stored as the universe claims the awareness as its food.

Matus doesn't credit Darwin's Theory of Evolution. He would say that species don't evolve because accidental mutations happen that prove to be advantageous and then become permanent changes. Individual beings change during their lifetimes as they enhance their awareness. A change in awareness is a change of the position of the assemblage point, which implies a change of being. Species-wide evolutionary changes are a matter of the entire species intentionally choosing a new position of the assemblage point after individuals point the way.

10

CONSERVATIVES AND LIBERALS

There's no way to know how we originally fixated our assemblage point, because it happened before we had identity, language or even thoughts. We can, though, become aware of how we maintain it in one place. We fixate and steady it through a constant internal dialog, which is a process of imposing our ongoing personal history on life with our thoughts and habits. The main part of this process is a never-ending chattering of thoughts, which becomes autonomic; we do it without being aware of it or in control. We can't stop it with conscious effort, because that effort is made up of more thoughts.

Because the assemblage point is stabilized in one place through a process of inner dialog and language, the way to dislodge it from its customary position on the cocoon is to quieten that internal dialog. This is the silence Castaneda is referring to in the title, *The Power of Silence*. If we want to free our assemblage point from the one spot we are accustomed to, we must achieve internal silence.

THERE ARE two types of knowledge: our every-day knowledge that comes from the use of language and reason, and silent knowledge which exists separate from language. During its history of life on the planet, which science tells us could be a million years or more, humanity was not always in the position of the assemblage point it occupies now. The current form of internal dialog we use to maintain our modern position is a relatively recent development in human history. Humanity has gradually moved from a place of silent knowledge to a place of reason. At a critical point, very recently compared to humanity's overall time on earth, silent knowledge was abandoned and reason and language took over.

We still have both parts in our being. One part is 'extremely old, at ease, indifferent. It was heavy, dark, and connected to everything else ... It was equal to anything. It enjoyed things with no expectation.' This older part of man did not need language; it proceeded the era dominated by reason and by thinking and writing in language.

The older side of man knew things that we no longer have access to. Knowledge and language are separate; we still have silent knowledge, but it's buried. It's drowned out by the chatter and clamor of our internal dialog. We can't access it using language; we can only point towards it. As we developed language and expanded our use of it, we lost access to the vast realm of silent knowledge. Every rational attempt we make to bridge the gap only increases the gap.

The modern rational part of man is 'light, new, fluffy, agitated. It is nervous, fast'. According to Castaneda, whereas the old part of man would look at a wilderness or empty field and not care to change it, modern man would want to cultivate rows of plants to feed people, or build something.

Ancient man knew what to do without thinking, not differentiating himself from nature. Gradually, the idea of an individual-self appeared, so he could predict and organize his doings. This individual-self first developed spoken language and, later, written language. Progressively, his thoughts, spoken and written words were used to 'dictate the nature and scope of man's actions'. Language was used to delineate and control man's range of activities and awareness.

Gradually the individual-self became stronger while connection to the ancient silent knowledge was lost. This loss of connection created a sense of hopelessness, which then started further mental activity to enhance or repair the self, to recover the feeling of connection. Because it was based on reason, this further mental activity could only increase the movement away from organic silent knowledge towards the individual-self.

Modern man now has an obsessive concern with himself. He has moved the assemblage point to an extreme position. As far as self-concern goes, modern man has moved to a position where the most extreme expressions of self-concern dominate his consciousness. There are extrinsic reasons for this movement, and it is a challenge facing humanity, imposed from outside ourselves by forces from the universe.

Because we are in the most extreme position of self-involvement, a pinnacle, any subsequent move of the assemblage point in any direction can only be away from self-concern. In other words, man's challenge in our era is to free his assemblage point by reducing his preoccupation with himself.

REASON and silent knowledge are two points. In our current era, our first point is reason. Everyone is near that point, but not everyone is squarely on it; most people are located somewhere between reason and silent knowledge. Those who are squarely on the point of reason are the true leaders of mankind. According to Matus, these are generally unknown people who have a genius for reaching and understanding the precise assemblage point position. They then influence the entire cohort, which is like the leader's audience.

In an earlier time, the first point was on silent knowledge, and the true leaders were squarely on that point. Mankind spent the vast majority of its history on the side of silent knowledge, which explains our great nostalgia for it.

It is only by arriving squarely on either position – reason or silent knowledge – that one can see the other position clearly. That's how the age of reason came into being. 'The position of reason was clearly seen from the position of silent knowledge.'

The goal of don Juan Matus and the new seers is to touch both positions using two one-way bridges.

'The one-way bridge from silent knowledge to reason was called "concern". That is, the concern that true men of silent knowledge had about the source of what they knew. And the other one-way bridge, from reason to silent knowledge, was called "pure understanding". That is, the recognition that told the man of reason that reason was only one island in an endless sea of islands.'

THE CONTENT and nature of perception are determined by the position of the assemblage point. In our era, the common position of the assemblage is the position of extreme self-involvement. According to Matus, self-reflection, self-concern, self-pity and self-importance are virtually the same thing. Our self-concern is the main force holding the assemblage point fixed.

Because we are in the most extreme position of self-importance, any sort of movement of the assemblage point will be a movement away from self-pity. Therefore, curtailing self-involvement is the way to free the assemblage point from its position. Through awareness of self-importance we can release the energy that's been used for it. Once the assemblage point has been released, it will move to another position on its own, away from self-pity and self-concern.

The movement of the assemblage point is defined as sorcery. If we reduce self-importance, the assemblage point will move. Where it moves is determined by universal intent. This is a real force that exists within the filaments of the universe which all beings are connected to. We cannot see it, but like gravity and electro-magnetism, which are also unseen, universal intent exists.

The assemblage point can be accidentally moved by illness, war, hunger, love, hate and mysticism, but any new position reached accidentally cannot be sustained.

Matus could intentionally move his own assemblage point and those of others. He could temporarily free Castaneda's assemblage point from its customary place, and influence it to move to another position, to teach Castaneda about other positions. Moving the assemblage point releases the energy that is being used to hold it steady.

Movements of the assemblage point can be large or small. They can also be very tiny movements, and reach 'isolated islands of perceptions', which are memories, either individual or shared. Information is stored on islands of perception. Human interactions are magical events that happen when strings from two or more luminous beings interact and intertwine. The universe is composed of uncountable positions of the assemblage point, where aware energy strings are combined. Events in our lives are 'experiences in the complexity of awareness'.

Life events are stored and can be revisited by moving the assemblage point back to that precise position. This causes the experiences to be relived. Many events from childhood are normally forgotten, but can reappear and be experienced again in great intensity and detail. During psychotherapy, the goal is often to reopen a forgotten event which has unresolved conflict or stress; to relive it and thereby neutralize its ability to cause ongoing anxiety and negative behavior. In our individual lives, we store and hide entire experiences so they are almost impossible to reopen.

Juan Matus took the idea of psychotherapy to its logical extreme. One of the most important facets of Matus' sorcery training is called 'the recapitulation'. Every apprentice is required to take time away, usually several years, to re-visit and re-live every event in his previous life.

According to Matus, the luminous body constantly sends out very fine filaments which are energized by feelings and emotions. In an interaction with another cocoon, each person sends filaments into the interior of the other's cocoon. If the interaction is not fully resolved when the cocoons part, each party leaves filaments inside the cocoon of the other person or persons involved. In this case, both parties lose energy to each other.

As human beings go through life they accumulate foreign filaments in their own cocoon. These left-behind foreign filaments are emotional assertions from other beings acquired during interpersonal conflicts. They become the basis for intrapersonal conflict, where we are in conflict internally with ourselves. They are the fuel for our chronic flares of self-pity and self-importance. The long-term effect of these exchanges is a loss of energy and a loss of freedom.

In Matus' recapitulation process, these past events are re-lived with a clarity and intensity that can be greater than what was felt during the original experience. Once an event is brought into focus and re-experienced, breathing consciously allows the luminous being to eject the filaments left inside itself by others. At the same time, it can retrieve its own filaments that it left inside the other beings that were in that event.

Mothers and fathers generally foist so much of their hopes, fears and expectations onto their children that the parents are left with actual holes in their energy bodies. These can be repaired, and the energy recovered. Children are not injured by having their parents' filaments removed from their luminous spheres.

We also inherit islands of stored experiences from our parents or caretakers. When we are infants our internal dialog hasn't developed yet and our assemblage point still moves freely. By unintentionally dreaming together with parents or caretakers, by simply spending time with them, we can encounter their stored experiences without speaking.

Ancestral, family and tribal memories can be passed on unknowingly when interacting luminous beings dream together. As babies, our assemblage points are completely fluid and haven't settled yet into position. Our parents or caretakers can pass on the locations of assemblage points, which are part of the universe's endless collection of 'islands of perception'. According to Matus, because of this sharing, we all have access to many islands of past experiences of family, tribe, country, and even the sorcerers of antiquity.

Works of great art can also move the assemblage point. Poems, statues, monuments, music and dance can all be among the highest forms of sorcery. They can bring us to a position of the assemblage point that the artist or builder knows about.

Advertisers, salesmen and politicians also practice forms of sorcery. Our perception can be changed in a positive or negative way, and we may or may not notice that we're being moved from one position of the assemblage point to another.

THE ABILITY TO retrieve energy from former acquaintances in the recapitulation process is another instance where Juan Matus' philosophy aligns with a famous conundrum in modern physics.

Matus said we can send energy to and extract energy from other luminous beings that are in unknown locations far away. The Principle of Quantum Entanglement explains that electrons in different places, seemingly not connected to each other in any way, can influence each other instantaneously. This would be normal in a universe of infinite strands of aware energy.

We could propose to go a step further and suggest that the quantum jump itself, where an observed heated electron jumps from one level to another instead of expanding smoothly, is the result of the duality of perception. Even using an electron microscope, scientists are still viewing events from the first attention. Therefore, there is a tiny gap in time and space between what is observed and the pre-perceived raw energy of the universe.

And, more generally, the reason light can be conceived as both wave and particle may also have to do with the first and second attentions.

11

LOST IN A DREAM

Castaneda's collection of literary work can be divided into four phases.

The first phase comprises the four books written during and just after don Juan Matus' lifetime. These recount Castaneda's thirteen years wandering the deserts and mountains of Mexico and Arizona with don Juan and don Genaro. This phase ended with Castaneda jumping off the cliff while Matus disappeared from the world. These four books were written as straightforward accounts from the first attention. Castaneda had adventures, took notes, and wrote what happened to him.

The second phase was the next four books. Written after don Juan's disappearance, roughly between 1975 and 1990, these told the story of Castaneda's return to Mexico, his reunion with the remaining apprentices, and his efforts for over a decade to remember the forgotten events and lessons from his time with don Juan. The topic was the process of discovering the second attention and recovering memories left there. Recovering memories from the second attention opened Castaneda to the totality of himself, which imparted new meaning to his previous life.

The Art of Dreaming, published in 1993, 20 years after Matus' disappearance, is the third phase. In this book, he described his final adventures and misadventures with Juan Matus in the second attention, remembered through the practice of dreaming. These events ended with a transition to the fourth phase of his life and work, when he moved back to Los Angeles.

IN DON JUAN'S PHILOSOPHY, there are two basic types of sorcerers: dreamers and stalkers. Sorcery is the ability to move the assemblage point. Dreamers achieve this through becoming aware of the natural movement of the assemblage point while dreaming, and then stabilizing their awareness at any new position discovered. Stalkers do this by modifying their behavior systematically until the new behavior causes the assemblage point to move.

Castaneda was a dreamer, and *The Art of Dreaming* is his most complete description of his speciality.

During our early life, we learn to immobilize our assemblage point at a position demonstrated and taught to us by our elders. Later in life, we rarely, if ever, allow it to move from its prescribed and agreed position. Normally, we are likely to fix it more precisely on one spot as we accumulate information during our life, which sharpens and hardens our focus.

Rarely, the assemblage point can be moved by illness or shock or other extreme emotions; if so, this results in extreme fear and disorientation, forcing us to quickly return to our accustomed position.

It's impossible to move the assemblage point by a conscious command, but it does move naturally during sleep and dreaming. According to Matus, the ancient sorcerers developed techniques to take advantage of that natural movement of the assemblage point to develop our perceptual abilities beyond their normal capacities.

Matus said that we can encounter the other self and bring it closer to our normal awareness through an enhanced type of dreaming. He taught this to Castaneda, who described the learning curve he had to navigate to become proficient. Juan Matus said dreaming was the only teaching method developed and prescribed by the ancient sorcerers to learn to use the second attention and reach the other self.

He warned, however, that dreaming was 'the most dangerous facet of the sorcerers' knowledge ... sheer dread, a veritable nightmare'. The path of dreaming led to ultimate tests for explorers of consciousness. The world of dreaming is a 'two-way hatch' between our world and other worlds.

Earlier in his training Castaneda discovered that every seemingly casual walk in the desert, or encounter with a merchant or stranger in a city market, could instantly morph into a matter of life or death. When he was with Matus, the world was filled with unknown power.

While learning dreaming Castaneda faced dangers that were 'enhanced a hundredfold', once the belief had been irrevocably shattered that dreams are just something that happen while we sleep.

DREAMING IS the only time in our normal lives when our assemblage point detaches from its fixed position and moves to other positions. Matus' philosophy suggests that this is the meaning of, and reason for, sleep itself.

Why must we sleep and dream? Why can't we just close our eyes and rest our bodies? Why must we go into a partly unconscious state to fully rest? Is it because what we are resting is the unconscious autonomic system that holds our assemblage point in place and keeps our awareness focussed? Maintaining our normal steady state of consciousness requires a major effort. Without realizing, we are fully engaged in this effort during all our waking hours. We need to lapse into some form of semi-conscious sleep state to rest from that effort. We don't really rest until the assemblage point is temporarily released from its fixation. After that we are refreshed and can start again. Without real sleep, we go insane.

Once our jabbering thoughts quieten down, we sleep. Our assemblage point releases and reverts to its natural condition where it moves fluidly. As the assemblage point moves, it aligns different groups of emanations of awareness from the universe, and we dream. We are conscious of some of our dreams but not always, and sometimes we remember them but mostly we don't.

As the assemblage point moves deeper into dreaming, it shifts further away from our normal thoughts and language. We enter the area of silent knowledge, where things are experienced and known without language. Sometimes, we get stuck in a gap between language and silence, and want to speak or yell but only noise comes out. As we later awaken from that state language reasserts itself. Our thoughts using language restart and the dream disappears from awareness because it's beyond the scope of language. If we don't note the dream quickly using words it's forgotten. We forget we have dreamed, or remember we dreamed but forget about what.

If we train ourselves we can gradually become more conscious of our dreams as we dream them, and of the transitions into and back from dreams. We can also train ourselves to remember more. This is often prescribed during various types of psychotherapy or hypnotherapy, to recover feelings, images and symbols that can be used to understand and improve our everyday behavior. However, according to Castaneda, this type of psychological analysis of dreams has limited value. It keeps us trapped in our world of self-reflection. He says it's possible to use our dreams to go beyond that.

MOST OF US are usually unaware of the process of falling asleep. We're not aware of our dreams starting and finishing, and then we wake up abruptly and forget everything, or almost everything. To make use of dreaming, Matus first taught Castaneda a three-step process. He taught him to be aware of the transition of falling asleep and entering a dream; then showed him how to hold the images in his dream steady; and finally trained him to remember the dream when he woke up. These three steps make up what Matus called 'crossing the first gate of dreaming'.

While awake we are in the first attention. While sleeping and dreaming we go into what Matus called 'dreaming attention'. This is an intermediate step to the second attention, and belongs to the realm of awareness after the first gate of dreaming opens. It's like a river that leads to an ocean, which is the much larger second attention. After passing the first gate, we are in a river leading to the second gate of dreaming. Beyond that second gate is the ocean, the full-on second attention.

The first attention normally must not be allowed to be aware of the second. Becoming cognizant of awareness being handed over from waking consciousness to dreaming must be done from the dreaming attention, not the first attention. There are no prescribed procedures that can be designed by the first attention to do this. It is simply intended – consistently and repeatedly. The dreaming attention will achieve it gradually through consistent practice.

In normal dreams we usually encounter many disconnected images which aren't necessarily assembled into a coherent world. We also don't consciously enter the dream and become aware that we are in it before something happens. Matus taught Castaneda to pause upon entering a dream, to arrange his attention, and to assemble the world inside that dream. This was done by moving his attention from item to item in the dream.

With repeated practice, a dreamer can focus on items in a dreamed world the same way we focus on items in our awake world. He can learn to allow all the items in a dream to arrange themselves into a world by glancing from item to item quickly. Without doing this, the dreaming attention tends to gape at anything. If we focus intensely on one thing, that object, which is only energy, will morph into something else. The dreaming attention needs to learn to serve the function of a beckoner, just as our first attention does. It needs to invite or summon the world in front of it to gather itself into an orderly world.

After passing the first gate of dreaming by learning these processes, it's possible to enter a dream and hold the images steady in the same way we hold images of our normal world.

While doing this, it's possible to discover our operative self in the dream, which Castaneda calls the 'energy body'. This is a 'ghostlike counterpart of the physical body'.

The energy body is the other self, or the double. It's in the second and larger part of our total awareness, which is divided by the two-step process of perception that creates our everyday awareness. Dreaming is the practical way of reaching the double. The other self, or the energy body, is composed, as we are in normal awareness, of energy. But it lacks the agreement to have mass and to be tethered to our normal physical world.

Castaneda said it took him two years of constant practice to pass the first gate of dreaming, at which point he became aware of falling asleep, could hold images in dreams, and his consciousness could enter his energy body. After that, his dreaming practice involved further training to develop and use the energy body. It must be perfected to the point that it has some control over the dreaming attention, to make it stop and return to normal awareness when needed.

Developing and using the dreaming ability depends ultimately on how we use our energy during our waking hours. We have a fixed amount of energy available to us in our luminous being. At any given time, at whatever level we're acting and perceiving, we are always expending all of our available energy. We arrange all of our energy to maintain our world and identity by keeping our assemblage point steadily fixed in one position, through our thoughts, habits and doings. We don't have extra energy, unless we re-arrange our habits and thoughts, and get rid of unnecessary items.

To have the energy available for developing our dreaming body and exploring realms made accessible while dreaming, we must free up energy normally used to deal with our normal, engulfing daily world. If our normal awareness is overloaded with routines, heavy emotions and fears about the self, then when we dream our freedom will be curtailed by symbols of those fears and concerns. We won't have the energy needed to cultivate awareness and volition in dreams.

Energy must be freed up using the recapitulation technique. When a dreamer finds himself unable to progress further, he must return to the recapitulation, the extreme form of psychoanalysis described earlier. He must unearth more life memories where his energy has been lost and foreign energy left inside his luminous being. Eventually, he will eject enough foreign filaments and recover enough of his own lost energy to proceed again.

Passing through the first gate of dreaming seems safe and harmless. In this area, though, we become aware of the astounding fact that we can have awareness in the world of our dreaming attention. We can encounter our energy body and learn to exercise it. According to Matus, we then gradually become aware that among the multitude of items in our dreams 'there exist real and energetic interferences, things that have been put in our dreams extraneously by an alien force'. Those alien forces are there to interact with us.

Matus said 'dreams are, if not a door, a hatch into other worlds ... dreams are a two-way street'. Our awareness can go through that hatch into other realms, and visitors and emissaries from other realms can come through the hatch to meet us in the dreaming attention.

Dreamers are still relatively safe in the area just beyond the first gate of dreaming, but it's an area filled with scouts and explorers from the next area, which is the full second attention. They come to meet us for the same reason we are there making ourselves available to them. We are all travelers and explorers in a universe that wants to know itself. We are the means by which the universe knows itself.

In our usual fragmented, half-remembered dreams, there are many elements that are simply images and memories from our daily life. There are also items that seem irrational or out of place, but when we look deeper and analyze them we see they are symbolic of things from our waking life. This is the area where psychoanalysts work. But in our normal dreams there are also many random items that make no sense and do not relate to our normal life, even symbolically.

We are usually unaware, but during dreams we are bombarded by visitors from the unknown. These onslaughts come from the next realm that dreamers can enter beyond the second gate. It's a dimension full of various other energetic beings. Some are entities that also inhabit our earth; others visit from further away. They do not physically come to us, but they can project their energy bodies into our dream attention and appear to us, just as we can go into our energy bodies and appear to them in their dream attention.

These scouts are perpetually curious about us. Like us, they are in search of more awareness and energy. When we dream, we enter a world where alien entities can reveal themselves to us. They send explorers to look for dreamers who are developing their awareness, and we are doing the same.

When focussing on evolving our dreaming attention, we expose our intent and our newly enhanced awareness to them, showing it off, making it accessible to them near their realm, like bait.

The alien entities cannot be the first to initiate an encounter with us while we are in dreaming attention. We are still protected by our walls of perception. It's only when we initiate contact that they are then able to engage and interact with us. They encourage us to accompany them into their world in the second attention. It's solely up to us whether we want to follow them or dismiss them.

After the first gate of dreaming attention, but before the second gate, we are still protected by our normal barriers. Until we pass through the second gate, we can still believe that we are 'only dreaming', albeit in an enhanced form. Even in this intermediate realm, though, there is a danger of being suddenly shocked. A foreign awareness could frighten us into an abrupt wakening, and then follow us into our daily world 'through the channel of fear'. It's possible for foreign energy to enter our world and be stranded, intruding in our life; it's also possible for our energy body to enter their realm and get trapped or lost.

BECOMING adept at the basic techniques of dreaming is arduous; it took Castaneda more than two years of continual practice to reach and then cross the first gate. But crossing the second gate of dreaming, into the vast and dangerous area beyond, can be simple. We just need to have the conscious intention to do it and state it aloud in our dream, or we can lie down in dreaming attention and fall asleep again with the intent of dreaming onward from there.

Crossing the second gate of dreaming implies the ability to change dreams without waking up, which means falling asleep into one dream and waking up from another. This can also be done by following a scout from dream attention to second attention by expressing the intention to do so.

By crossing this boundary the dreamer enters a more vast and dangerous kind of attention. In this realm, the dreamer learns about the rules and customs of sorcery dreaming. He encounters fateful challenges to his sobriety and unavoidable tests of his intent and focus. He doesn't always realize where he is, or what he's doing, or what the stakes are.

According to Castaneda, the area beyond the second gate of dreaming is the realm where we first begin to encounter the other kinds of sentient beings that share our planet.

About two-thirds of the energy inside the human cocoon belongs to the realm of the unknown. The other third is energy and awareness that we can access, the 'human band'. The energy inside the human band is organized into 48 bundles. We use only two of these for our normal first attention, in order to perceive all the animate and inanimate objects in our world.

Six other bands out of the 48 belong to a realm of sentient beings that share the earth with us, and partially share our perceived world. Some of these beings hover in our dreams, seeking contact with us.

These beings also have energetic cases of energy with assemblage points. Our cases are spherical, and our energy level shines much more brightly. Their energy cases are long and candle-shaped, and shine more dimly. They see more than we do, as their longer shape touches more varieties of universal energy than our sphere does, but they see with a dimmer light.

The total population of these inorganic beings is less than the total number of organic beings we normally perceive in our two customary bands. But the variety of types is higher because they occupy six bands to our two. They differ from us in that they have awareness but they don't have organisms. Their life span is infinitely longer than ours; Matus believed their remaining life spans match the earth's. Their energy level is much lower. They have already been alive for eons, and will live eons longer, while our lives are much shorter, but much more intense.

They live a stationary existence, like trees rooted to one place for an unimaginably long time. In their first attention, these beings without organic bodies and processes live as stationary objects. Because they are stationary in their first attention, they have overdeveloped their second attentions, which they are experts at using. They have energy bodies like we do, which are also not tethered to the world of their first attention.

Of the 48 bundles of aware energy in our cocoons, only two belong to our normal world, while six belong to the world of these inorganic beings. Their world's awareness is partially connected to ours, like a one-way sound-proof mirror. They look at us, envying our energy level, but they can't contact us on their own volition. We are normally completely unaware of them, although we sometimes sense their presence.

Beyond the six bands that compose the inorganic partner beings' world, there are another forty bundles which, combined, contain at least another 600 worlds. For human explorers of awareness to visit those many worlds, they must first pass through the inorganic beings' world, getting a boost of energy from that realm needed for further travels in awareness.

ONCE WE ENTER the second attention we are compelled to interact with these beings. If we follow them to their world, they appear to us 'very much like a giant sponge':

'The first thing it did was to push me through a huge cavern or opening into the physical mass I had been facing. Once I was inside that mass, I realized that the inside was as homogenously porous as the outside but much softer looking, as if the roughness had been sanded down. What I was facing was a structure that looked something like the enlarged picture of a beehive. There were countless geometric-shaped tunnels going in every direction ... The tunnels seemed to be alive and conscious; they sizzled.'

The inorganic beings are immobile, but have awareness that is much more sophisticated than ours because they are much older. Being immobile and infinitely experienced, they seek to influence things that move around them, and they covet the higher energy levels of humans.

When a dreamer is in the dreaming attention, he is in the realm where the inorganic entities of our earth operate in their second attention. They use their energy bodies to create projections when dreamers appear in that realm. The inorganic beings seek out dreamers and basically try to capture them. They cannot force a dreamer to do anything, and they can't lie. But they can read many of the dreamer's innermost feelings, and create images and projections to entice or frighten.

They get our attention by projecting images into our second attention because they want to interact with us. They are motivated to interact with us, and when we become dreamers in another realm we are also bidding for enhanced awareness. We become avidly social, seeking out individuals and groups of foreign awareness.

Compared to them, we are like small children with lots of energy but no sophistication. They know we are vulnerable, and with their vast knowledge and long history of life on our planet they can easily manipulate us through curiosity, pleasure or fear. They want to entice us to enter their world and voluntarily take up residence there.

The decision to stay in that world must be voluntarily made by the dreamer. Once made, it is irreversible, and the dreamer can be imprisoned in that world. That means he dies in his normal awareness and becomes an inorganic disembodied being living an infinitely long life in that realm.

Don Juan called the inorganic beings, and the way our awareness interacts with theirs, diabolical. But there was nothing he could do to help Castaneda make his decision about what to do in their realm. As a dreamer, Castaneda needed their instruction to develop his dreaming practices and their energy for further travels in awareness in the more exciting and perilous areas beyond their realm. He had to decide on his own to either accept or reject the offer of safe asylum they make to all dreamers.

Making it even more diabolical, dreamers are taught and helped by the inorganic beings. As soon as a dreamer develops some proficiency, he encounters a 'dreaming voice' which informs and teaches him. This voice comes from an inorganic being, and is very helpful, informative, and honest. Since ancient times this voice of dreaming has taught humans the way to navigate in the second attention.

Don Juan tried to teach Castaneda how to deal with the seemingly invaluable information given by the inorganic voice. In fact, the voice can only disclose information which the dreamer already has stored in his second attention. We're drawn to the inorganic beings because of their 'superb consciousness'. They seem to know our innermost thoughts and needs because they are vastly older and more experienced. At the same time, they have an ulterior motive in relating to us.

Every dreamer must pass through this realm and make an individual and final decision in response to the inorganic world's appeal. Once a dreamer decides, completely on his own volition, to reject their appeal he is then free to travel on to the exciting but dangerous second attention. If he ever voices his desire to stay in their realm and live an infinitely long life, he enters a safe, closed world; his decision is final, and he can never leave.

The ultimate appeal of the inorganic beings is that their world is like a refuge for humans who travel in the second attention. The worlds beyond the inorganic realm are even more predatory and hostile to us than our own is. Gains in awareness are only achieved after life-or-death struggles in unknown realms. Our partner world of the inorganic beings is a safe place.

In fact, our partner world, always there next to us behind its one-way mirror, is the ultimate home of the ancient sorcerers. According to Matus, the sorcerers of antiquity became overly involved with the inorganic beings and the dreaming voice. They assumed those beings were working in their interest, helping them wield power over their fellow humans.

It was the inorganic beings and their projections that originally taught mankind about the assemblage point and how to manipulate it, through their relationship with the ancient sorcerers. The ancient sorcerers mistook those projections to be helpers or protectors, and referred to them as their allies. Ultimately, Matus told Castaneda, 'every sorcerer of antiquity fell, inescapably, prey to the inorganic beings. The inorganic beings, after capturing them, gave them power to be the intermediaries between our world and their realm, which people called the netherworld.'

Don Juan Matus told Castaneda that after years of exploration beyond the allies' realm he now felt revulsion toward
both the ancient sorcerers and the inorganic beings, who he
called 'our first cousins'. 'The energy from our first cousins is a
drag,' said don Juan. 'They are as fucked up as we are.'

Castaneda knew that if he was to be one of the new seers he
had to first retrace the steps taken by the ancient sorcerers, but
then at a certain point take a different path to seek freedom.
Matus warned him repeatedly that he saw that Castaneda had
tremendous affinity with the old sorcerers and the inorganic
beings. In the end, despite Matus' warnings, Castaneda
succumbed to the lure of the inorganic beings' world and was
taken captive.

Castaneda carried on a long courtship with this netherworld, which he kept secret from Matus. Finally, Castaneda was
baited with the image of an imprisoned, helpless and innocent
child, also called the 'blue scout'. Taking the bait, Castaneda
disappeared into that world to rescue the phantom child. That
should've been the end of his story, but Don Juan and his
cohorts found and rescued him, and brought him back to
Mexico, with the blue scout catching a ride along with him.

Castaneda was then totally spent of energy, and had to rest
in bed for months, while Matus and the other sorcerers
debriefed him and helped him recover. They were shocked to
hear his story; according to don Juan and his companions,
Castaneda somehow visited an area of the inorganic realm
known about since ancient times, but never visited before by
any of them. Not only that but none of the ancient sorcerers'
stories mentioned going to that area either. Castaneda's story of
his capture and rescue in the 20th century was now part of the
ancient sorcerers' folklore.

THE NEXT STEP in Castaneda's training was to cross the third gate of dreaming. This involved merging two realities: the dreaming reality and the reality of the daily world. The moment of falling asleep usually acts as the effective barrier between awake awareness and dreaming awareness. Our waking awareness is normal and predictable, while dreaming is unusual and not predictable. Normally, it's quite rare for someone to find himself in a state where he isn't sure if he's awake or in a dream.

After years of training, though, Castaneda's dreaming body could now move about at will. He shifted worlds repeatedly in dreaming, and eventually found that items from his dreams came into his daily world. He was in a position where he didn't always know whether he was in normal awareness, in a normal dream, or in a dangerous and unknown dreamed world.

With scouts from other realms stalking him, ready to whisk him off to unknown realms, and inorganic beings trying to suck him back to their world, it became imperative for Castaneda to always know what he was confronting. He had to know whether any being he met was just a neighbor from down the street or an unknown power from another realm likely to attack him for no reason, as he might kill an insect scurrying across his desk.

Some may say we are stranded in our world of daily life, with our assemblage point so fiercely attached to one place that we're unable to remember that we came from somewhere else with a purpose. Similarly, dreamers and sorcerers can wander into worlds and forget where they came from and why. Matus told stories of some cohorts who went into other dark and frightening worlds and became stranded, seemingly for decades, and then returned to this world where they learnt they had, in fact, been gone for only a few days. Like Castaneda in the world of the inorganic beings, dreamers can fall, intentionally or accidentally, into many situations, even some that are worse than death.

There are dark images throughout Castaneda's work of sorcerers and would-be sorcerers who became trapped in prolonged or endless misery. This came about either through their own selfish quests or because they were victimized by others.

According to Juan Matus, sorcerers through the ages have attempted to discover ways to prolong life and extend their awareness, with some of the ghoulish results described by Castaneda. Few of those depicted seem like positive achievements, and most appear worse than death. Various types of failed 'death defiers' appear in Castaneda's work.

These dangerous and confusing currents built up momentum as Castaneda approached the fourth gate of dreaming, which led to the last episode in *The Art of Dreaming*. This would be the final apprenticeship story Castaneda recounted in Mexico.

After passing the fourth gate of dreaming, the energy body can travel to specific pre-selected places, either in a real world or in the intent of others. In other words, it is possible to be sent to a place by someone else. Matus said that traveling to a place defined by someone else's intent is both the most difficult and dangerous dreaming exercise. It was also 'by far, the old sorcerers' predilection'.

Matus revealed that one of the favorite pastimes of the primitive old sorcerers was to effectively sell their apprentices into slavery in another realm in exchange for power or energy. By the time the apprentice reached the point where he could travel in someone else's intent, his teacher could then manipulate him into a realm that the teacher knew about and leave him there, stranded in the unknown. The ancient sorcerers were known to move entire groups of people into other worlds.

In another pivotal event of Castaneda's apprenticeship, he met an old sorcerer who had lived for untold ages, perhaps thousands of years. This old sorcerer was known as 'the death defier'. Like all ancient sorcerers, he had been trapped in the inorganic beings' world, but somehow found a way to escape and retain his prolonged existence as an inorganic being without being confined as a prisoner in their realm. He escaped by changing his gender to female. According to Castaneda, in the second attention, the universe is predominantly female, and because of its rarity the male element is valued. But gender is a position of the assemblage point, so a male sorcerer can conceivably change to female by finding the right position.

This ancient sorcerer became part of don Juan's lineage by returning to the same church in Mexico in each generation of sorcerers to compel the lead sorcerer to trade: energy for the death defier in exchange for knowledge for the sorcerer and his cohorts. Over thousands of years this sorcerer from antiquity had witnessed ancient times on earth, as well as faraway reaches of the universe, so she had many secrets to reveal.

As leader of the new generation, Castaneda was required to meet the ancient sorcerer, known also as 'the woman in the church'. In a gesture of false generosity, he declined to receive any gifts from her. He said he only wanted to be taken for a walk in don Juan's town as it was 300 years ago when the death defier first contacted their lineage.

Because she had spent almost an eternity living in that area, she had a clear image of the town square, church, streets and houses as they were hundreds of years ago. Once Castaneda crossed the fourth gate of dreaming, he could take a walk with her in that town as it existed in her memory, so he did.

On the return trip from the past image of the town, the woman took her gift, the exchange she was still entitled to, from Castaneda without announcing it. She brought him on a side visit to another place. She tricked Castaneda into believing she had simply returned him to the real town they started from in normal awareness, when, in fact, she was still escorting him around in her own memory. In this state, she managed to bring one of Castaneda's new cohorts, a woman named Carol Tiggs, into the dream with them and then effectively kidnap her.

Assuming he had been gone for two days and one night, Castaneda woke from this adventure and found don Juan and his cohorts waiting for him. They somberly informed him he had been missing for nine days, not two. When he told his story, they concluded that the death defier managed to take Carol away with her to join in her destiny – hopefully to go into the third attention with Castaneda and his party.

Castaneda was told that he again had managed to delve into realms of dreaming and sorcery previously unfamiliar to Matus and his lineage. Castaneda had added yet another unprecedented chapter from modern times in the accounts of the ancient sorcerers of Mexico.

12

COMING DOWN IN L.A

C astaneda's story about his captivity and subsequent rescue from his path-breaking explorations of the second attention is yet another abrupt disconnect in his chronology. Thinking through his whole body of work again, we passed through the psychedelic stage first. After that came the stage of the warrior encountering his double and leaping into the unknown. Then, he returned to Mexico and put the myth of the ancient sorcerers in place. Finally, he got himself lost and then found again in frightful dreaming journeys. Now, we discover that he used these last episodes of dreaming as a hatch to launch himself through with a new group of apprentices into another realm: Los Angeles.

With boundaries collapsing within and around him, Castaneda again re-arranged his ensemble of characters and recast the story of himself, the famous sorcery apprentice. It all now became the lead-up and introduction to the next and final phase of his personal history in his favorite place in any world: Los Angeles.

At this point for most readers, Castaneda has pushed his conceit too far, and it starts to unravel from the complexity. To insist that Castaneda really had all his adventures with don Juan and the shifting troupes of apprentices, and then managed to land on his feet a famous and wealthy man in Los Angeles with a harem of beautiful and powerful women and a crowd of followers exalting his every utterance, gets too difficult to believe.

In retrospect, the most likely scenario of what happened would be along these lines: Castaneda wrote his first book in the 1960s to start his PhD candidacy at UCLA and establish himself as an anthropologist. He had access to original information from an ancient religious and sorcery tradition whose dogma introduced him to the concepts of the first and second attentions.

This tradition was common in wide areas of the world in ancient times. There would've been numerous written or oral accounts defining the precepts of this proto-religion and telling stories of its saints and followers. These accounts would have been severely repressed during the Inquisition, so anything that remained would've been secret. This original information could've been formal treatises on the religious precepts, or diaries or myths depicting the activities of real or mythological heroes of the tradition. Castaneda's originality and effectiveness in depicting activities of 18th- and 19th-century characters in Juan Matus' lineage might place the origin of his sources in that era.

Castaneda could have made the fateful decision while writing the first book, to defraud UCLA by inserting himself into the story he had found. He could've invented the character of don Juan based on information given to him by anthropologists he had talked to at UCLA as an undergraduate. And he then inserted himself in the role of apprentice.

Perhaps, he had planned that his first book, *The Teachings of Don Juan: A Yaqui Way of Knowledge*, would be circulated and debated amongst anthropologists in academic journals only, and be enough to result in an eventual PhD and career as professor of anthropology. When the book became wildly popular instead and a worldwide bestseller, a whole new world of options, both lucrative and treacherous, appeared.

Once it was clear to Castaneda that the first book was bringing critical acclaim and financial rewards, what harm could there be in writing a few more? The possibility of turning the story of don Juan the sorcerer into an epic myth from ancient times extending into the 20th century may have slowly dawned on Castaneda.

He could have composed the first three books based on interviews with local informants in Mexico who knew some old stories. Once he became acquainted with the philosophies of the double and the second attention, endless possibilities of storytelling opened to him. In this scenario, his fraud would broaden and deepen until it became too unwieldy as it uncontrollably intertwined with his personal life back in the first attention in the USA.

At the same time, under this scenario his literary accomplishment would have to be called amazing. And to have the Florinda Grau Donner and Taisha Abelar books published in 1991 and 1992 alongside his still-thriving career was fantastic.

IN THE INTRODUCTION to *The Art of Dreaming* (1993), Castaneda mentioned three new female sorcery apprentices as his new partners, and promised to write later of their adventures and concerns. In other words, he said that there was a second group of co-apprentices who had joined him and don Juan, roughly between 1970 and 1973, presumably after Matus realized the first group of apprentices had become unworkable. This rationale is difficult to square with his earlier writing, but is plausible. This new group consisted of only three women.

The implication is that he must have only met the members of this group in the second attention before 1973. That would mean he had no memories of any of them until they gradually re-appeared in his first attention more than a decade later. He became re-acquainted with them at various times between 1981, when he mentioned one of them briefly, and 1993, when he introduced all three in *The Art of Dreaming*.

The first was Carol Tiggs, who he also called the 'nagual woman'. She was referred to as Castaneda's female counterpart and co-leader of the sorcerers of his generation. Juan Matus reportedly recruited her in Tucson, Arizona, shortly after he met Castaneda. She was working in a government office where Matus had gone to get some documents processed. He pretended to be a helpless native American confused by bureaucracy, and visited her repeatedly for three months until he tricked her into visiting his house.

As nagual woman she should have left the world with Matus and his group in 1973, but that didn't happen. The new story says that before that could happen, she got mixed up in Castaneda's dreaming adventures, both in the inorganic realm and then again with the ancient sorcerer who appeared as the woman in the church. Instead of following Matus and his cohorts Tiggs disappeared with the death defier.

The other two newcomers were Taisha Abelar and Florinda Grau. They were never properly introduced in Castaneda's books. Instead, they wrote their own.

Castaneda had his epic story of being a modern sorcerers' apprentice augmented, affirmed and expanded by not one but two other authors. They each depicted themselves as characters on parallel journeys to Castaneda's, and in their renditions they have all the players meet and interact on several levels of awareness. For Castaneda the writer, this can only be called a literary triumph.

Castaneda, Grau and Abelar all attempted to direct these three versions of the story through one hatch into the contemporary historical world. They all met up in Los Angeles. They set up a business as well, and recruited new followers. Along with readers from two decades before, everyone tried to understand and accept the new regime, which inevitably created contradictions.

Castaneda's rationale for introducing the new apprentices, Grau and Abelar, so late, in 1993, had to be based on a claim that they had been together between 1970 and 1973. They only interacted in the second attention, and, therefore, forgot about each other.

But Grau said she had visited Castaneda in Los Angeles countless times, and had driven with him repeatedly to Mexico and back to Los Angeles, and had the keys to his place, in 1973. Were they doing the three-day drive from Los Angeles to Mexico in the second attention? We learned later that immediately after his jump from the cliff in 1973, Castaneda returned to his apartment at UCLA. Why didn't he and Grau find each other at his place in Los Angeles during all those years after 1973, when he was at the height of fame and she had the keys?

Florinda Grau, later known as Florinda Donner, was a German who grew up in South America. She said in her book *Being-in-Dreaming* (1991) that she was taken to live for many months in Juan Matus' house in central Mexico with his group of old sorcerers. This was in 1970, while she was at UCLA, but before she knew anything about Carlos Castaneda.

She said she was first exposed to Castaneda, unknowingly, in a scene set up by Matus. He intentionally put a dead insect on her hamburger in a coffee shop in Tucson to create a confrontation between her and Castaneda, who was posing as the cook named Joe Cortez. A year later, in 1971, she met him again as Joe Cortez while hiking on a foggy hill near Los Angeles. Then, she went to a Carlos Castaneda lecture on the UCLA campus. She saw him onstage and recognized him and went backstage to meet him.

Castaneda suspected there was some extraordinary connection between them. He invited her to accompany him to the sorcerers' house in Mexico, not knowing that she had already been there. When they arrived, she was joyfully reunited with the sorcerers' group. She became part of the learning cycle of Castaneda's generation, with him as the leader. According to Grau, Castaneda used many aliases, as part of his attempt to be what Matus called a 'stalker': besides Joe Cortez, he was also known as Charlie Spider and Isidoro Baltazar.

Grau said she was tutored mainly by the female members of the older generation. Her training as a female sorcerer differed from Castaneda's. As a woman, she was automatically much more fluid in dreaming. Her learning focussed on using the womb as the main locus of power and intelligence. She said she didn't seem to need to endure the years of doubt and questioning, tricking and cajoling that characterized Castaneda's training. Dreaming on many levels came naturally to her. On the other hand, she barely wrote about the underlying philosophies of the luminous being and assemblage point.

Castaneda said the main difference between male and female apprentices was that 'male warriors must be given serious reasons before they safely venture into the unknown. Female warriors are not subject to this and can go without any hesitation, providing they have total confidence in whoever is leading them.' Another way to explain this is that men have more sobriety and sense of purpose, while women have more pure talent and intensity.

Grau said that she drove with Castaneda to Mexico on his final journey to see Matus on the day that the old sorcerers were leaving the world. They drove together, but she stayed at the sorcerer group's home while Castaneda continued to the plateau where he jumped from the cliff. He never returned for her; she was left with several of the old sorcerers who stayed behind.

Abelar's book, *The Sorcerers' Crossing*, was published in 1992, a year after Grau's book. Abelar said don Juan Matus discovered her in 1960 in Tucson when she was only 15. Looking for the men's room at a drive-in theatre, Matus accidentally entered an employee's area and interrupted Abelar as she was about to have sex with another employee. He was so shocked at the unlikeliness of the encounter that he considered their meeting an omen. He had his female cohorts keep track of her over the years until finally sending one of them to pick her up and bring her to Mexico.

Abelar spent years living in the sorcerers' house with two

teachers, a caretaker and large dog named Manfred that was also a sorcerer (the same dog that helped dona Soledad trap Castaneda). She met Juan Matus in Mexico several times.

Abelar's training consisted mainly of recapitulation, the technique of remembering whereby memories are reviewed in the first attention while a deep breathing exercise cleanses the energetic residues of the remembered interactions. She was also taught 'magical passes', physical movements designed to re-route energy in the body and the double.

During most of her training, she slept in a tree house and suspended from high branches in elaborate harnesses. Abelar was told about Castaneda, the 'new nagual', but never met him. She saw him from a distance once with Matus' entire group.

She said: 'Four of the men were older and looked as fierce as the nagual, but one was young. He had a dark complexion; he was short and seemed very strong. His hair was black, curly. He gesticulated in an animated way as he talked, and his face was energetic, full of expression. There was something about him that made him stand out from all the rest. My heart leapt and I as instantly drawn to him.'

AFTER *THE ART OF DREAMING*, five years passed with no books, before *Magical Passes* appeared in 1998. In the introduction to this book, Castaneda said he had accepted his fate that he was not capable of continuing and passing on don Juan's lineage. After 27 generations, Matus' lineage was ending with him. Because Castaneda was not going to pass on the knowledge to a secret group of new sorcerers, he decided that his task was to find public ways to disseminate the knowledge instead.

Castaneda had written nine books up to this point. He had finished remembering all the teachings that he was capable of handling, and described them in writing. But one piece was missing: the *Magical Passes*, the last secrets he was carrying. He decided to take this final piece of secret knowledge and formulate it into a modern collection of martial-arts-like exercises and market them with a brand name: Tensegrity.

Castaneda explained that the magical passes were not invented, but discovered by the sorcerers of ancient times. He said that 'while they were in states of heightened awareness, their bodies moved involuntarily in certain ways, and that those certain ways ... caused ... an unusual sensation of physical and moral plenitude'. Don Juan felt that these movements were something like 'a hidden heritage of mankind' left in our bodies to be discovered in order to ease the extreme stresses of the warrior's path while also making the body pliable and strong.

Castaneda said Matus taught him that the body has six main centers of vitality. The duress and stress of everyday life pushes energy away from these centers. The unused energy gathers on the periphery of the luminous sphere, where it hardens into a shell. Performing the magical passes breaks up this encrusted energy and returns it to the body's centers of vitality.

The six main centers of vitality are listed in order of importance: the area of the liver and gallbladder; the pancreas and spleen; the kidneys and adrenals; the hollow spot in front of the neck; the womb; and the top of the head.

Castaneda said that the center of energy at the top of the head had been taken over by a foreign power, and had a foreign energy in it. 'The sixth center of energy,' he said, 'doesn't quite belong to man. You see, we human beings are under siege, so to speak. That center has been taken over by an invader, and unseen predator. And the only way to overcome this predator is by fortifying all the other centers.'

Once the new female apprentices were introduced, we never again see the old Castaneda-as-apprentice. The note-taking, doubting, questioning, non-seeing, frightened and confused student who acted as a foil for Juan Matus and Genaro Flores in the early books is gone. Castaneda is now the 'young nagual', the leader of the new generation. As for his followers, old descriptive words like student, cohort and apprentice are now often replaced by a new word: disciple.

13

A YAQUI CONCLUSION

J uan Matus told Castaneda that his native Yaqui Indian civilization, after several centuries of oppression, had been reduced to just a remnant of what it once was. Small bands of survivors held on in separate outposts spread across the Sonoran desert in Arizona and northern Mexico. Having lost their land to the Mexicans, and their way of life to the Spanish Conquest, Don Juan said that they were left with only their anger and self-pity.

Castaneda tried to enter a Yaqui town several times, but 'had been made to turn around by the sheer hostility of the people who lived around it'. Government bankers were the only outsiders normally allowed into town because they bought all the crops from the Yaqui farmers.

Don Juan brought Castaneda into the town once while in the second attention. Even though he couldn't speak Yaqui, he felt he received a clear message from them:

'*Those people were indeed warlike. Their propositions were propositions of strife, warfare, strategy. They were measuring their strength, their striking resources, and lamenting the fact that they had no power to deliver their blows. I registered in my body the anguish of their impotence. All they had were sticks and stones to fight high-technology weapons. They mourned the fact that they had no leaders. They coveted, more than anything else one could imagine, the rise of some charismatic fighter who could galvanise them.'*

Juan Matus said that his defeated and humiliated tribe, the Yaquis, epitomized the worldwide human condition of our age. We feel defeated, humiliated, and left powerless by a monstrous outside force that governs and ruins our lives. This is the one thing that unifies humanity, according to Matus, that we all have in common. All humans have the same sense of outrage, offense, self-pity and grievance – even billionaires and presidents.

In every book written by Castaneda, don Juan Matus returned to this theme and hammered on it. The primary characteristics of mankind in this era are self-pity and its concomitant self-importance. These are consistent and universal characteristics of humanity in our era. It's true for all adult humans alive on the planet right now regardless of location, race, creed or status. Our interior dialog, which stabilizes our world view, is full of recitations of problems, unfulfilled expectations, misunderstandings, frustrations and endless grievances. We are trapped in this dialog, and don't even conceive that there could've been another type of consciousness in the past or could be another type in the future.

If the story of human awareness is compared to a river, Matus said that we have become trapped in a small eddy, and moved into a shallow side pool of the main river, where we spin endlessly, going nowhere. He said this is a temporary condition imposed on us from outside.

In the earlier age of silent knowledge, as opposed to today's age of reason, a different realm of awareness and knowledge existed along with a different kind of human. Matus' religion ruled then, and its leaders were men and women who we now call sorcerers. Their arena of activity in the realms of awareness was much vaster than ours is now. It was undeniably a much darker time, as well.

Once the position of reason was clearly seen, mankind started moving in that direction, away from the primal connection with nature and the arbitrary dominating power of the old sorcerers. The age of reason brought new rulers with a new kind of power from technology.

According to Matus, this movement from an era of silent knowledge to an era of language, science and reason has also been accompanied by an occupying invader from another area of the universe of aware energy. As we moved to a form of awareness closely circumscribed by reason, leaving vast parts of our total being unused, a predator took advantage. It moved in, unseen, to take our neglected awareness, which is the vast majority of our total awareness, as its food.

It's striking that Castaneda waited until his final chapters of his last book to introduce this predator, called the 'flyer', but he did include several clear but undefined and unexplained portrayals of it in earlier works. He said the presence of the 'flyer' explains why we use such a small part of our total being to live our lives and so little of the power available to us, and why we perceive such a small portion of what should be our birthright as creatures in a universe with many worlds in it.

Why is it that we have vast realms of consciousness and

awareness within our beings, but are kept cut off and in denial
of them? Why do we identify exclusively with our dreamed self
and deny the dreamer, our double, which is the vaster part?
How can we live a double life, but only remember one part of it,
the smaller part?

According to Castaneda, we are trapped in this condition
because it has been imposed on us from outside by this invis-
ible invader from another realm. This monstrous and malevolent predator from somewhere in the vast reaches of the
universe has taken us prisoner. It lives with us and feeds on our
awareness, controlling us by imposing its own mind on top of
ours. It's a smart and organized species of half-visible predator,
an inorganic being from our twin world that has succeeded in
turning 'man, the magical being that he is destined to be ...
[into] an average piece of meat'.

We are kept like livestock, and repeatedly stripped of our
awareness. In an ingenious process, the predator takes the best
part of our awareness and leaves us only the part that flares up
with self-pity and self-importance. These impotent flares are
also consumed in a repeating process that generates hopelessness and impotent fury. Like prisoners serving an impossibly
long sentence without even knowing what their crime was, we
direct our energy onto fighting over what meagre status and
privileges we are allowed in our prison.

This predator somehow installed its own mind on top of
our natural mind. Being a secret predator engaged in a nefarious activity, this predator mind is conspiratorial, cunning,
furtive, evasive and insidious. Most of all, it is afraid of being
discovered and exposed. Because the predator has installed its
mind onto us, we believe that its fearful and paranoid feelings
and concerns are our most important feelings and concerns.

When we take steps to remove the predator from our lives, we fear the wrath of a higher justice, because those are the concerns of the predator itself. It is deathly afraid of being caught and exposed in its nefarious doings, and then deprived of food.

Just as repeated exposure is needed when we view the mould of man to get beyond the first impression where we are awed and overwhelmed by the glory of our own archetypal image, so it is with the 'flyer'. Repeated exposure to the predator is needed to get beyond the extreme horror, fear, guilt, hopelessness and impotence we feel on first encounter.

When the 'flyer' is faced repeatedly with a silent mind it goes away. Inner silence, the opposite of inner dialog, makes us indigestible to the predator.

When the predator departs our awareness returns. We can recover our coat of awareness, our sheen. According to Matus, that is 'the toughest day in ... life, for the real mind that belongs to us, the sum total of our experience, after a lifetime of domination has been rendered shy, insecure, and shifty. Personally I would say that the real battle ... begins at that moment. The rest is merely preparation.'

This fearsome monster that rules and imprisons us is an integral part of the universe, just as we are. Humans are sophisticated 'energetic probes created by the universe'. Through us the universe intends to become aware of itself. The monsters who imprison us are our challengers. There is no other way to look at them. If we take them as such, we can continue.

14

GRANDFATHER AND ANTOINE

Having to believe is not the same as simply believing. We think we live in a world of reason. There is also the world of will and power. According to Matus, the most dangerous time is when the world in front of us is neither one nor the other. When this happens the way forward is to act as if one believed. To move forward we must believe without believing, but that does not exonerate us from thoroughly examining our situation.

One of Castaneda's earlier stories, from *Tales of Power*, illustrates this: the story of Max the cat. A friend of Castaneda found and raised two abandoned kittens. Several years later, she sold her house and was unable to take the cats with her or give them away. Her only option was to arrange for the cats to be taken to an animal shelter and put to sleep. Castaneda volunteered to be her driver.

He parked outside the animal shelter. His friend picked up one cat and carried it into the facility. While this cat was being carried, it played with the owner, purring and pawing her gently.

Castaneda looked at the second cat, Max. In an instant, he saw that Max knew exactly what was going on and had no intention of allowing himself to be carried off. Max growled, hissed, and hid under the seat. After making some half-hearted attempts to catch him, Castaneda opened the car door and yelled, 'run, Max, run!'

Max was suddenly transformed 'into a true feline' and bolted from the car, racing low to the ground across the street and along the gutter until he found a large storm drain and dove into the sewer.

Castaneda told this story over and over to his friends, and gradually developed a pleasurable sense of identification with Max. Castaneda was sure that he, too, although he might be like a spoiled and pampered house pet, could someday be over-taken by the 'spirit of man', and would at that ultimate moment choose to dash off in a final definitive journey.

It's not enough to simply believe the most felicitous option, Matus told him. You cannot simply dismiss the second option, that the cat might've been drowned or killed within minutes of his dash for freedom. It's one thing to have a single shining moment when the spirit takes over. To be prepared for it and to sustain it, though, is another matter.

There is still another option to be considered. What about the other cat? Naturally, we want to identify with Max, but what about the possibility that we might instead be like the other cat that happily allowed itself to be carried off to be destroyed, still filled with its house-cat illusions?

For us to make a final judgement about the veracity and value of Castaneda's work, we also must straddle two worlds where it's neither one nor the other. Firstly, we could simply believe Castaneda's story at face value, that he met don Juan in Arizona in 1960 and carried on exactly as written. In the books, Castaneda has given us at least two strong hints to reject that option. He endorsed Florinda Grau's contradictory story about her interaction with him, and he inserted the story of Antoine the plagiarist on the last pages he ever published.

The second option is to pounce on these contradictions, and Castaneda's failures of annotation and corroboration, along with other concerns that may exist outside of Castaneda's texts. We then judge the author to be a shameless fraud, a trickster and huckster of the lowest type, whose blatant and willful dishonesty undermines and disqualifies all his writings. His ideas, therefore, should also be deemed unworthy.

If we want to assert a positive value to Castaneda's work, without allowing Castaneda to trick us, we have to believe a third option. We have to believe that the story of Antoine was Castaneda's deathbed confession. That means, of course, the author himself did not live the life described in the Castaneda books. He somehow plagiarized someone else's work to produce the long epic with the characters of Carlos Castaneda, don Juan Matus, and all the other sorcerers and apprentices.

Perhaps, the author discovered an old unknown manuscript telling the story of another Castaneda and don Juan, either real or imaginary, from another time. Or, maybe, he knew a storyteller who knew the story of an historical don Juan, or who recited stories from a tribe's oral tradition.

In either case, perhaps Castaneda initially put himself into the story as the main character, not foreseeing the incredible popularity that would eventuate and entangle him hopelessly. Success after success forced him to carry on and extend the falsehood, initially for just two or three more books, and then for decades, until the sheer weight of the deception became too much and, for many readers, the myth started to break up.

Regardless of whether the work is authentic or fiction, or authentic but plagiarized, what is its value? How good is the story? Those are the questions remaining, we have to believe.

IT'S NOT easy to imagine the kind of 20th-century childhood and upbringing that would create an author who could write the entire epic story of Castaneda and don Juan, whether fact or fiction. We would have to imagine a child brought up in an unfettered way, raised by a benign and detached family in the countryside, both unregimented and unsheltered. He would live in a country somehow existing out of time, full of historical characters but somewhat separate from the global upheavals of that era. He would have come of age as a mixed-national Westerner during the Second World War without being affected by it.

Castaneda provided many anecdotal set pieces from his early life, and in his final book, *The Active Side of Infinity*, he added more. He said his mother left him when he was very young, so his school-teacher father sent him to be raised on his wealthy grandfather's farm somewhere deep in South America. Castaneda called it an ideal situation, in that he was raised by a father who he described as 'considerate, tender, gentle and helpless' and a more powerful grandfather.

Consequently, he was mainly left to his own devices. As a boy, he roamed his grandfather's farm. When a white falcon terrorized their chicken coop, Castaneda spent weeks stalking the bird, but when he finally had his chance and raised his rifle and took aim, he decided not to shoot the magnificent creature.

He boldly made friends with his grandfather's archenemy, Leandro Acosta. Acosta was a homeless drifter, whom his grandfather often accused of burglary. He lived in the woods and made his living by various means, mainly by trapping live animals to sell to collectors. After several hunting expeditions together, Acosta proposed that the eight-year-old boy help him with the most exciting challenge: to catch a live vulture. This involved sewing the boy inside the gut of a dead donkey to wait for the king vulture to descend and eat the donkey. All went to plan, and when the vulture tore open the donkey's body and stuck its head inside, Castaneda grabbed it by the neck and managed to hold on long enough for Acosta and his helpers to capture the bird.

At nine years old he played billiards extremely well. When a criminal friend, Falelo Quiroga, became aware of this, he bribed the boy with coffee and Danish pastries. He put him up against local billiard sharks at midnight matches with high-stakes gambling. When he first met Quiroga, Castaneda introduced himself as Carlos Aranha, his preferred name as a boy. Quiroga would send one of his thugs to help the boy escape from his bedroom for each contest, catching him when he jumped from the window. They won match after match, with Quiroga promising to put money in the bank for the boy. Finally, he demanded that Castaneda throw a match, and intentionally lose by one point. If he refused, the scary thug threatened some undefined punishment. Castaneda became confused and couldn't answer. His grandfather was somehow alerted and saved him by moving the whole family to another town far away.

In his new town, he rafted down the river when it was in flood with his friend Crazy Shepherd. They ended up stranded on an island for eight days as the river raged. People from the town floated rafts to them with supplies to keep them alive.

A year later, when he was ten, his fishing buddy, Sho Velez, dared him to raft again, this time on an underground and unexplored river that went into a cave and through a mountain. Velez' somewhat unhinged father was planning to do it by raft, which would have been fatal. To save the father, the two boys stole the raft, entered the cave, and floated on the strong current into the middle of the mountain. They ended up in a deep still pool with no visible exit, and no way to go back. Castaneda dove down and found a hole near the bottom which drained the pool. With no other choice, both boys left the raft and dove into the hole and ended up going down a water chute until they emerged clear on the other side of the mountain.

Crazy Shepherd and Velez were the only people in town who Castaneda considered to be alive and vital; they had courage. 'No one else in that whole town had any. I had tested them all. As far as I was concerned, every one of them was dead, including the love of my life, my grandfather.'

Decades later, Don Juan insisted that Castaneda unburden his consciousness of all his important memories, either to thank the protagonists who shared his positive experiences, or to rid himself of negative residues from unhealthy ones.

Castaneda's grandfather compared him to his two similar-aged cousins. Alfredo was handsome and spoiled by his good looks, and would always be invited to every party. Luis was homely and not too smart, but honest. He would rarely be invited, and would stay home. According to his grandfather,

Carlos was a son-of-a-bitch, neither good nor bad, and would generally be shunned, but would crash every party any way.

For a time, around age 14, Castaneda lived with an aunt whose house was haunted by ghosts. Eventually, someone sent him to Italy to study sculpture. While there, his Scottish friend, Eddy, introduced him to the unforgettable aging prostitute, Madame Ludmilla.

His next memory is of two friends from junior college, Patricia Turner and Sandra Flanagan, who were best friends. He managed to get both of them to fall in love with him at the same time. A bit later, he got engaged to Kay Condor, an aspiring actress; he liked her because she was blond and a head taller than him. His friends came to the wedding, but Condor left him standing at the altar; she couldn't go through with it.

Castaneda's professors and employers are also part of his recapitulation. But the last, and top billing, is saved for his grandmother, who he suddenly introduced, and now asserted that she was the real power behind his benevolent grandfather. In fact, there's really no reason for this story to be told, especially at the very end of his last book and very near the end of Castaneda's life.

His grandmother rescued a local indigenous man who was about to be lynched by her employees, accused of sorcery. This rescued sorcerer became her servant. He advised her to adopt a newborn orphan and raise him as her own son, angering and alienating her large family. She sent the adopted son, Antoine, to Europe to study. In his early thirties, he returned to visit her during a time young Castaneda was staying with her.

Castaneda and his grandmother described Antoine as 'dramatist, theatre director, writer, poet'. They both repeated the assertion that while the entire family were corpses that walked, Antoine was alive. His only unfulfilled desire was to have talent and be a 'writer of note'.

Antoine wrote, directed and acted in an acclaimed play at a local theatre. For months, performances were successful until suddenly he was denounced in a newspaper and his work proved to be plagiarized. The grandmother was in denial and continued to back her adopted son, accusing the entire town of profound envy.

Days later, the grandmother called Antoine for a meeting. She said she was dying and had no time left, but encouraged him to carry on and live. At the advice of her sorcerer-advisor, she had sold all she owned and transferred all the proceeds to Antoine. She implored him to leave immediately before the family came to take revenge. Antoine packed his trunks, called a car and driver, and made one last stop at grandmother's front door before leaving. He recited a new original poem, which she immediately accepted as his plagiarized yet valuable offering, and sent him on his way back to Europe.

We have to believe Castaneda wanted us to treat him the same way his grandmother treated Antoine.

15

TWELVE BOOKS, THIRTY YEARS

To get an idea of the range and scope of Castaneda's total works, and how his underlying ideas are introduced and illustrated, here are brief synopses and summaries of the twelve books. Castaneda's philosophy of achieving full awareness through memory, and the interplay of the first and second attention, can best be understood in the context of his story that unfolded over a long time. Dates are included to show the chronological context of books and historical events.

BOOK 1: *The Teachings of Don Juan: A Yaqui Way of Knowledge* (1968)
SYNOPSIS: Castaneda meets don Juan in a bus station. Introduction of concepts of *diablero* and *brujo*. Don Juan's family history. Dates of initial apprenticeship: 1960 to 1965. Three 'power plants'. Power objects. Corn sorcery and allies. Finding

the best sitting spot on the porch. Eating peyote and playing with the dog. Devil's weed. Four enemies: fear, clarity, power and old age. Picking peyote. Meeting Mescalito. Finding a path with heart. Datura and lizards. Datura and flying. The little smoke takes your body away. Mescalito singing in a luminescent peyote field. Sea kelp. Devil's weed as a spy. Two lizards. Becoming a crow. Last encounter. Lost and regained his soul.

SUMMARY: The first book, published at the height of the 1960's political upheaval in the USA, was the introduction of Castaneda and don Juan. Their first meeting in 1960 was described. Some of Matus' friends and relatives were introduced. Matus' instruction in the growing and using of 'power plants' – peyote, datura and mushrooms – was also explained. Don Juan decided to take Castaneda as his apprentice, but after five years Castaneda freaked out, feared he was losing his mind, and withdrew from Mexico in 1965.

BOOK 2: *A Separate Reality: Further Conversations with Don Juan* (1971)

SYNOPSIS: The difference between seeing and looking. *Sacateca* dances. Boys outside the restaurant. Don Vicente, three people at a car, and a wasted gift. Allies. *Mitote*. *Bacanora* for Lucio. Meeting Eligio. Thinking. Seeing the death of don Juan's son, Eulalio. Meeting don Genaro. Nestor and Pablito, his apprentices. Don Genaro on the waterfall. Gnat guardian of the other world. Don Juan's parents. Castaneda's promise to 'button nose' boy. Don Juan's benefactor can't see. Spirit of a water hole. Green fog and bubbles. Traveling in water. Smoking an ally. La Catalina. Shields. Holes in sounds. A bout with power. Following don Genaro.

SUMMARY: Castaneda returned to Mexico in 1968 and restarted his relationship with don Juan. Don Genaro Flores was introduced as Matus' sidekick and the long apprenticeship wandering the desert began to be described. The paradox of awareness was introduced, where it is imperative that we protect ourselves from the inexplicable forces of the universe. If that is all we do, we lose our birthright as humans, as perceivers capable of magic. The difference between looking and seeing was explained and demonstrated.

BOOK 3: *Journey to Ixtlan: The Lessons of Don Juan* (1972)
SYNOPSIS: Don Juan explains about stopping the world. Agreements. Making a fog around yourself. The right way of walking. An omen. Talking to plants. The white falcon. Death as our advisor. Taking responsibility. Castaneda's father. Hunters. 'Of course we're equals.' To be available and unavailable. Stop being prey. Magical deer. Last act on earth. The trapped rabbit. Becoming accessible to power. Dreaming. Being buried. Trapping a mountain lion. Control and abandon. Lightning in fog. The cave. The bridge in the fog. Sunset dance on a hilltop. Entities of the night. Shadows. Four warriors make a ring of fire. La Catalina. Don Genaro makes Castaneda's car disappear. Stopping the world and talking to a coyote. Don Genaro on the road to Ixtlan.

SUMMARY: Don Juan no longer used 'power plants' to help Castaneda. Castaneda's awareness was now opened and his shields brought down; he had to learn to live like a warrior so he could explore the unknown while protecting himself from its assaults. Castaneda learns about erasing personal history, losing self-importance, death as an advisor, assuming responsibility, becoming a hunter, being inaccessible, disrupting the routines of life, the last battle on earth, becoming accessible to power and the mood of a warrior. Dreaming was introduced as the safest way to expand awareness.

BOOK 4: *Tales of Power* (1974)

SYNOPSIS: Don Juan explains the importance of personal power. A moth in the bushes. Calling 48 friends. Don Genaro. The double. In two places at once. The double tries to urinate. Story of don Genaro's double. The double dreams the self. Genaro calls the ally. Eight points of luminous fibers – two epicentres: reason and will. Don Juan in a suit and tie. Having to believe. Max the cat. A dying man in Alameda Park, Mexico City. The tonal and the nagual. Items on the table. Looking at tonals. Don Juan shoves Castaneda through the airline office. Genaro flies through the trees. Pablito, Nestor and Genaro. Explaining the teachers' strategy. The bubble of perception. Reflection on walls. Practice jumping. Meeting the four allies: black rectangle, giant coyote, thin man and black jaguar. Hurled up and down. The sorcerers' explanation. Jumping from the cliff.

SUMMARY: Castaneda learned to encounter his other self, his double. The double was explained, and how it exists because of our two-step process of perception. The double is encountered in dreaming, and then we learn that it is the double that dreams us – this is the mystery of the dreamer and the dreamed. The eight points of our being were explained, and how we normally only use two of the eight points. The tonal and the nagual were also introduced as the known and the unknown, as was the island of the known and its importance.

The sorcerers' explanation was given, and how it led to the events on the high plateau in 1973, when Castaneda jumped from the cliff.

BOOK 5: *The Second Ring of Power* (1977)

SYNOPSIS: Castaneda drives on Pablito's new road. Dona Soledad's new floor. The dog in the car. The touch of the double. The 'little sisters', Lidia, Josefina, La Gorda and Rosa, arrive. The double strikes Rosa. Curing Rosa and Soledad. The double comes out again and La Gorda enters. In the cave. Calling the allies. The human form. The 'Genaros' – Pablito, Nestor, Benigno and Eligio. Toltecs. Pablito's chair. Discussion of their four jumps. The Art of Dreaming. Children and completeness. The 'little sisters' perform. Josefina's gift. Castaneda remembers. The second attention. Tonal and nagual. Gazing. Two faces.

SUMMARY: Castaneda returned to Mexico looking for explanations. Instead, he wandered into a struggle for power amongst the apprentices. The 'Genaros' and the 'little sisters' were introduced. Castaneda injured and then cured three of them, but they discovered Castaneda couldn't lead them. Castaneda could see for the first time.

BOOK 6: *The Eagle's Gift* (1981)

SYNOPSIS: Castaneda visits the pyramids at Tula. Objects of fixation of second attention of ancient sorcerers. Looking for Matus and Genaro Flores. Dreaming and seeing together with La Gorda. The saber-toothed tiger. Feuding apprentices go to the city. Silvio Manuel's house. Crossing the bridge. A wall of fog. Going separate ways. Castaneda loses the human form in Los Angeles. Remembering the nagual woman. Who runs Castaneda, Juan Matus or Silvio Manuel? The barren landscape of sulphur dunes. Limbo. Remembering movements between the first and second attention. The rule of the nagual. Four types of men and four types of women. Julian takes don Juan to church. Don Juan's courtship of Olinda. Don Juan's party of 16 warriors. Castaneda's party of eight warriors. Castaneda and La Gorda break the rule. Silvio Manuel tries to help. Castaneda loses energy and then revived. Florinda and Celestino. Castaneda's vow with dona Soledad. The plumed serpent.

SUMMARY: The apprentices split up and went their separate ways. Castaneda and La Gorda, working together, learned how to remember the other self and how to move back and forth between the first and second attention. They dreamed together and discovered shared memories in the second attention. Learning to move from the first to the second attention was the teaching method used to arrive at the totality of one's self. Castaneda remembered and started to tell the narrative of the ancient sorcerers of Mexico, the Toltecs. The new seers were defined, with their new version of the Toltec religion. Memories of our luminosity were also explained.

BOOK 7: *The Fire from Within* (1984)

SYNOPSIS: Heightened awareness and remembering are discussed. Toltec seers. The new seers' lineages began around 1600 AD. Don Juan's lineage consisted of 14 naguals and 126 seers. A new beginning noted in 1723; the eight following naguals were different from the six preceding. Petty tyrants.

Don Juan and the foreman. The eagle and its emanations. Sexual energy. The inventory. Inorganic beings. The mirror in the water. The nagual's blow. The shape of the cocoon. Running with La Catalina. The mastery of awareness. Julian and his changes. Seeing people and the tumbler. Sebastian and the death defier. The four seers and their court. The mould of man.

SUMMARY: Teachings for the right side and left side were now explained, and Matus' group of 16 sorcerers was introduced. Also described were the mastery of awareness, the summation of don Juan's teachings; the agglomeration of energy fields; the luminous sphere; and the assemblage point where perception is assembled. The eagle and the universe's intent were explained, where perception arranges other worlds and beings at positions of the assemblage point. The mold of man was described, and its importance. Ways of dying were noted, including burning from within. And Castaneda depicted how the eagle loans us awareness and eats our enhanced awareness when we die.

BOOK 8: *The Power of Silence* (1987)

SYNOPSIS: Matus' teacher Julian, and his teacher Elias. Julian the tragic actor. Tricking don Juan. Meeting Vicente Medrano and Silvio Manuel. Seeing the emanations. The place of no pity. Don Juan leaves the nagual's house and has a family. Don Juan dies, and then returns to Julian's house. Stalked by a jaguar. Becoming gigantic. Here and here. Julian throws don Juan in the river. Two one-way bridges. Tulio.

SUMMARY: Silence means the cessation of the internal dialog; silent knowledge versus knowledge from language and reason. There are two parts of our being: the silent part – old, at ease and connected; and the modern rational part – light, nervous and fast. Ancient man was ruled by silent knowledge, and that era lasted much longer than our current one. The development of the individual self and language led to excessive self-concern. There are two points – silent knowledge and reason – with two one-way bridges between them. The assemblage point makes isolated islands of perceptions.

BOOK 9: *The Art of Dreaming* (1993)

SYNOPSIS: Introduction of Carol Tiggs, Florinda Grau and Taisha Abelar. Old sorcerers often changed their human energy shape. Don Juan takes Castaneda to a city out of this world. Interacting with inorganic beings. Relationships of annoying dependence. Secret meetings with the inorganics. The dreaming emissary and its advice. Scouts and tunnels. Elias and Amalia. A door called dreams. 'No one wants to leave.' The sad little girl. A mortal encounter survived. Recapitulation before the third gate. Attacked on the street in Tucson. The world is an onion. Awareness is an element. Appointment with the tenant. Male and female are positions of the assemblage point. The woman in the church. Shouting in the second attention. Carol loses her lisp. Carol is gone.

SUMMARY: Dreaming is the only way to harmoniously move the assemblage point. It is also the most dangerous facet of sorcery. The first gate of dreaming is becoming aware of falling asleep, then holding a dream steady. Dreaming attention is the preliminary part of the second attention, like a river that leads to the sea, which is the full second attention. Matus explains the energy body. Dreaming is a two-way street, a hatch between worlds full of scouts from other realms. The second gate of dreaming is changing worlds inside a dream or following a scout. Castaneda encounters the other beings who share the earth with us. The inorganic beings and their historic role in dreaming are explained. They help dreamers, and have their appeal. The ancient sorcerers all ended up in their realm. Castaneda took the bait, was caught and then rescued. Later, Castaneda met the woman in the church, the death defier.

BOOK 10: *Magical Passes* (1998)

SYNOPSIS: Castaneda moves to Los Angeles with his three female cohorts, Tiggs, Grau and Abelar. There are six centers of vitality in the human body. One has been taken over by an invader, an unseen predator.

SUMMARY: Castaneda was now living in Los Angeles with his three female cohorts as the leader of a new, modern sorcery enterprise. He introduces magical passes, which were discovered by sorcerers of ancient times and were an integral part of his apprenticeship. Castaneda now made them available to all.

BOOK 11: The Wheel of Tine (1998)

SYNOPSIS: The meaning of time. Remembering the words of don Juan

SUMMARY: Passages from previous books

BOOK 12: *The Active Side of Infinity* (1999)

SYNOPSIS: Castaneda meets Madame Ludmilla. Bill drops Castaneda off at the Greyhound bus terminal. Jorge Campos and Lucas Coronado. Vitaminol, the cure for everything. The psychiatrist's knock. Pete and Patricia. Rodrigo Cummings goes to New York. The Great Garrick. Don Juan comes to LA. Professor Lorca. Patricia and Sandra. UCLA. Falelo Quiroga's deal. Catching a live vulture, playing billiards and rafting rivers. Luigi Palma. Alfredo, Luis and Carlos. Visiting the Yaquis. The aunt who walks at night. Ernest Lipton and his Volkswagen. Seeing all our lives. The 'flyer'. Humans are farmed like chickens and kept in human coops. Leandro Acosta. Sho Velez. Antoine. Ship's café.

SUMMARY: Castaneda's describes his childhood with his grandfather, his farm and his town. The 'flyer' is introduced and described, along with Castaneda's grandmother and her darling Antoine, the plagiarist.

REFERENCES

Abelar, Taisha. 1992. *The Sorcerers' Crossing: A Woman's Journey*

Donner, Florinda. 1991. *Being-in-Dreaming: An Initiation into the Sorcerers' World*

ABOUT THE AUTHOR

photo by Sulastri

Peter Luce was a school teacher in Philadelphia, and then worked for 30 years in the jewelry business between Bali and New York. He now lives in Indonesia.

For more information:
www.gettingcastaneda.com
PeterLuce@gettingcastaneda.com

If you enjoyed this book, please leave a review on Amazon.com so others will enjoy it too.

Printed in Great Britain
by Amazon

40350061R00108